Study Guide

for

Hardman, Drew, and Egan

Human Exceptionality
Society, School, and Family

Seventh Edition

prepared by

Keith W. Allred
Nevada Department of Education

Allyn and Bacon
Boston London Toronto Sydney Tokyo Singapore

A Pearson Education Company
75 Arlington Street
Boston, Massachusetts 02116

Internet: www.ablongman.com

ISBN 0-205-34446-1

Printed in the United States of America

10 9 8 7 6 5 4 3 04 03 02

Contents

Introduction

This study guide will help you learn the major concepts, principles, and vocabulary presented in the 6th edition of *Human Exceptionality*. It will also help you become a more effective learner. Research suggests that employing specific learning strategies increases comprehension and retention. This study guide has been formatted around a study skill known as PQ4R (Thomas & Robinson, 1972).

PQ4R consists of 6 stages: **Preview, Question, Read, Reflect, Recite,** and **Review**.

Preview. First read the chapter focus questions and the preview in this study guide. Then read over the section headings and subheadings.

Question. Develop questions related to your purposes for reading. If you can answer the focus questions in the study guide, you should be able to master the salient points covered in a chapter. If not, then you should have some very specific purposes to guide your reading.

Read. This is your first sweep through the text. The study guide lists most of the *terms* the authors have determined to be particularly important. Re-familiarize yourself with this key *vocabulary* to improve your comprehension; as you read, seek answers to the questions you read earlier.

Reflect. Ask yourself how each new fact or idea relates to what you already know. The purpose of reflecting is, in part, to make connections between new information and material you have previously learned. The "matching" exercise in the study guide provides practice in recalling what you have just read. You have read the material too quickly if you struggle with this exercise.

Recite. Reciting is another means of thinking again about what you have just read. After each section or subsection, pause and attempt to answer the questions that guided your reading. By completing the "fill in the blank" exercise, you will recite/recall many of the important concepts covered in the text. Noting how well you do in completing this activity is one means of checking your understanding of the material.

Review. Scanning the headings and subheadings is one form of review; answering the questions presented prior to reading is another. The "multiple choice questions" in the study guide also provide review. If you correctly answer these questions without referring back to the text, then you have some assurance that you have comprehended what you have read.

Let me express my admiration and respect to each of you for choosing education as your profession. As a teacher, some of your most fulfilling experiences will come as you work with individuals with disabilities

Chapter One

A Multidisciplinary View of Exceptionality

Preview

In Chapter One you will learn about ways that various professions view people with significant differences and about several approaches to labeling such people. The differences between abnormal behavior and social deviance are explained. An historical perspective regarding services for those with disabilities is presented, including various issues that influenced passage of federal laws insuring the educational rights of all children. You will find out the major mandated provisions in several federal laws for students with disabilities, including multidisciplinary and nondiscriminatory assessment of educational needs, parental involvement in developing each child's educational program, a free and appropriate public education (FAPE), education in the least restrictive environment, and development of an individualized education program (IEP). Several contemporary issues, including disciplining students with disabilities, School Reform, and Inclusive Education are discussed. Also conditions that affect the likelihood of students failing and/or dropping-out of school are described.

Question

As you read the chapter you should seek answers to the following questions:

What are the four major reasons why people are labeled?

What three approaches are used to describe the nature and extent of human differences?

What are four indications of quality supports and services for persons with disabilities?

What is the purpose of the Americans with Disabilities Act?

What services ensure that an individual with a disability will live and learn successfully within his or her community?

How have nineteenth century physicians/philosophers increased our understanding of people with differences?

How does one distinguish between abnormal behavior and social deviance?

What three things can we say about educational services for students with disabilities during most of the 20th century?

What three fundamental rights were affirmed by the courts leading to the enactment of Public Law 94-142?

What are the five major components of the Individuals with Disabilities Education Act?

What actions, under IDEA 97, may a school take when a student brings a dangerous weapon to school or is involved with illicit drugs?

How does one distinguish between students with disabilities who are eligible for services under the Americans with Disabilities Act and those who are eligible under IDEA?

What is meant by *inclusive education*?

What conditions are most closely associated with students considered "at risk"?

Read

Following are a number of the key terms used in Chapter One. Match each term with the phrase that most closely describes or defines it. You should complete this exercise before you read the chapter.

a. normal
b. labeling
c. handicapped
d. developmental approach
e. least restrictive environment
f. social inclusion
g. I.D.E.A.
h. students at-risk
i. nondiscriminatory assessment
j. social deviance
k. ADA
l. P. L. 94-142
m. exceptional
n. home school placement

1.1. ______ First major federal law insuring the educational rights of children with disabilities.
1.2. ______ Services provided in a setting that is consistent with the individual's need.
1.3. ______ The practice of using popular terminology to categorize people who differ from the accepted norm.
1.4. ______ Violation of the social norms of a particular group.
1.5. ______ Integration of people with disabilities into community settings.
1.6. ______ A term used to describe someone who is considered average.
1.7. ______ A person's ability to adapt to environmental demands.
1.8. ______ The most recent amendment to P.L. 94-142 entitled The Individuals with Disabilities Education Act of 1992?

1.9. ______ An approach to labeling based on deviations in the course of normal development.

1.10. ______ Testing procedures intended to be fair/impartial regarding students with disabilities.

1.11. ______ A comprehensive label for persons who need special services in school.

1.12. ______ Students not identified as disabled who still need the support of special services to succeed in school.

1.13. ______ Major civil rights legislation known as the Americans with Disabilities Act of 1990.

1.14. ______ The school the student would attend were she/he not disabled.

Reflect

This exercise is intended to provide practice in recalling what you have recently read. It will be most beneficial to you if you do not refer back to the text while completing it. As you match these items, consider how what you have just learned relates to other knowledge, concepts, and/or principles you have learned before taking this course.

a. ecological approach
b. I.E.P.
c. manifestation determination
d. John B. Watson
e. disorder
f. Jean-Marc Itard
g. disability
h. environmental bias
i. P. L. 99-457
j. parent involvement
k. educationally disadvantaged
l. cultural approach
m. continuum of placements

1.15 ______ Amendment to P. L. 94-142 extending education rights to preschoolers

1.16 ______ Theorist who believed that idiocy could be treated through educational

1.17 ______ Range of settings in which appropriate educational services are

1.18 ______ Role(s) and responsibilities of parents regarding their child's education.

1.19 ______ Approach to labeling that defines what is normal according to

1.20 ______ The influence of "setting" on one's perception of another person.

1.21 ______ Deliberation regarding whether a particular behavior is attributable to the student's disability.

1.22 ______ Students with "two strikes" against them from the start.

1.23 ______ An approach that views behavior as adaptation between person and environment.

1.24 ______ The means for providing educational and related services for a child with disability.

1.25 ______ Loss of function.

1.26 ______ Theorist who advocated that all human behavior is learned.

1.27 ______ Label referring to a malfunction of mental, physical, or psychological processes.

Recite

In this exercise you are to supply a word/phrase in order to make sense out of a statement of a concept, definition or principle that otherwise is incomplete or lacks closure. Several answers may be acceptable for an item; therefore, in comparing your answer to the one found in the key do not be overly concerned with having a word-for-word match. Instead, focus on whether or not your answer is equivalent to the answer that is supplied.

1.28 Everyone is in some way __________ from everyone else.

1.29 Labels tell us whether or not a person meets the expectations of the ___________.

1.30 Labels help professionals to _____________ more effectively with each other.

1.31 A range of behavioral and physical differences may be found in every ___________.

1.32 *Average* is a statistical term based on a large number of observations of

1.33 All people engage in a process of self-___________.

1.34 In the medical model, ______ is defined as the absence of a biological problem.

1.35 A widely used educational label for children is _____.

1.36 The educational label ______ has a negative connotation.

1.37 Abnormal behavior may be learned through the interaction of the individual with the __________.

1.38 The theory of social _______ led to widespread fear of people with disabilities and influenced a movement.

1.39 People cannot be held against their will and without treatment in an institution if they pose no threat to _________.

1.40 One harmful aspect of institutionalizing people with disabilities has to do with the diminished regard for individual ___________.

1.41 ______________ was reaffirmed as a right and not a privilege by the Supreme Court in the case of Brown vs. Board of Education.

1.42 The least restrictive environment concept indicates that an individual should receive services in a ___________ that is consistent with his or her specific needs.

1.43 A number of ________ contribute to increased labeling of students as educationally disadvantaged.

Review

In completing this last exercise you have the opportunity to review many of the major points in Chapter One. Please take time to consider which is the best response vs. a correct response. Doing so will increase your understanding of the material you have read.

1.44 One reason people are labeled is
- a. to aid the U.S. Census Bureau
- b. to reinforce the implied behavior
- c. to determine who is eligible for special services
- d. to determine who is normal

1.45 Unofficial labelers are
- a. court officials
- b. sanctioned by society
- c. behavioral scientists
- d. teachers

1.46 *Stupid*, *cripple*, *fat*, and *crazy* are:
- a. unofficial labels
- b. official labels
- c. medical terms
- d. psychological terms

1.47 Which approach to labeling reflects a view of human differences as the result of the interaction of biological and environmental factors?
- a. The medical approach
- b. The environmental approach
- c. The developmental approach
- d. The individual approach

1.48 The term *exceptional* describes individuals who
- a. are limited because of environmental demands
- b. have higher than average general ability
- c. are sufficiently higher or lower than the norm to require specialized services
- d. have a general malfunction of mental processing

1.49 Students who do not meet the educational expectations of society may be
- a. labeled according to the extent of their deviation
- b. labeled by the type of deviation they exhibit
- c. provided specialized services
- d. all of the above

1.50 According to the sociological approach, social deviance is
- a. not necessarily an illness
- b. necessarily an illness
- c. desirable in some societies
- d. usually inherited

1.51 The best definition of a handicap is
- a. a person's physical disability
- b. a general malfunction of mental processes
- c. limitations imposed on a person by the environment
- d. a disturbance in normal functioning

1.52 The major provisions of Public Law 94-142, as enacted in 1975, included
- a. the use of nondiscriminatory and multidisciplinary assessment
- b. a provision for all students to be educated with their nondisabled peers in general education classrooms and schools
- c. a plan for transitioning all students from school to adult life
- d. all of the above

1.53 Which approach to labeling deals with self-perception?
- a. The individual approach
- b. The personal approach
- c. The developmental approach
- d. The cultural approach

1.54 The least restrictive environment (LRE) requirement in I.D.E.A. states that individuals with disabilities should
- a. all be educated in general education schools
- b. all receive equal services
- c. all be educated with their nondisabled peers to the maximum extent appropriate
- d. all go to special schools

1.55 The purpose of the individualized education program (IEP) is to

a. provide an appropriate educational experience for each student
b. promote effective communication between school and parents
c. establish continuity in the delivery of educational services from day to day, as well as from year to year
d. all of the above

1.56 Which physician/educator, through his work with Victor the wild boy, demonstrated that individuals with severe disabilities can learn new skills?

a. John Locke
b. Louis Braille
c. Phillipe Pinel
d. Jean-Marc Itard

1.57 Which person advanced the idea that there is no basic human nature or knowledge and that our minds at birth are a blank slate?

a. Jean-Marc Itard
b. John Locke
c. Sigmund Freud
d. Ivan Pavlov

1.58 Special schools and segregated living facilities established during the early nineteenth century focused on which type of treatment philosophy?

a. Highly specialized education and training
b. Basic care and management
c. Vocational training
d. Individualized education and treatment

1.59 Which theory of the early twentieth century caused fear of people with disabilities and led to the passage of marriage and sterilization laws?

a. Abnormal behavior is a product of the environment.
b. Intellectual deficiencies are primarily fixed, incurable, and hereditary.
c. Intellectual deficiencies are primarily due to sociocultural factors.
d. Hereditary factors play an insignificant role in the cause of mental and social deviance.

1.60 Isolated residential facilities for persons with mental retardation are called

a. special education schools
b. integrational facilities
c. institutions
d. least restrictive environments

1.61 Which court case resulted in the first major court action on behalf of persons with mental retardation residing in public institutions?
   a. Halderman v. Pennhurst
   b. Youngblood v. Romeo
   c. Rouise v. Cameron
   d. Wyatt v. Stickney

1.62 The U.S. is moving away from institutionalization to more appropriate placements such as
   a. community-based settings
   b. state hospitals
   c. mental health centers
   d. asylums

1.63 The primary purpose of the ADA is to provide
   a. educational rights for all, regardless of disability
   b. a national mandate to end discrimination against individuals with disabilities
   c. services for those with disabilities who are not covered in Section 504
   d. recreation and leisure-time opportunities for individuals with disabilities

1.64 The major provision(s) of P. L. 99-457 is/are
   a. expansion of the law to include preschool children with disabilities
   b. an individualized family service plan, or IFSP
   c. establishment of state grant programs for infants/toddlers
   d. all of the above

1.65 The growing number of students "at-risk" includes those who are
   a. latch-key children with no after-school support
   b. living in single-parent families
   c. living below the poverty line
   d. all of the above

1.66 Definitions of *inclusive education* may include
   a. home or neighborhood school placement
   b. support networks or circles of friends
   c. both full and partial participation in the general education classroom
   d. all of the above

1.67 IDEA requirements for nondiscriminatory and multidisciplicary assessment testing procedures include
   a. testing all children in English
   b. the use of the IQ test as a primary tool for determining eligibility
   c. a team approach to assessment
   d. all of the above

1.68 IDEA gives parents the right to
  a. consent in writing prior to evaluation for special education services
  b. question their son or daughter's special education program and placement
  c. make recommendations about educational programming
  d. all of the above

1.69 The provisions for a free and appropriate public education (FAPE) are based on
  a. the Supreme Court ruling in Brown v. Board of Education
  b. the Mills Case
  c. the 14th Amendment to the Constitution
  d. Civil Rights Act of 1964

1.70 The major provision(s) of the ADA include:
  a. telecommunications
  b. public accommodations
  c. transportation
  d. all of the above

1.71 The principle of zero tolerance states that
  a. the consequences for a student's misbehavior are predetermined
  b. student's are permanently expelled after three infractions
  c. student's should be treated as adults for serious offenses
  c. students with disabilities must be treated like the non-disabled

ANSWER KEY FOR CHAPTER ONE

READ

1.1 l
1.2 e
1.3 b
1.4 j
1.5 f
1.6 a
1.7 c
1.8 g
1.9 d
1.10 i
1.11 m
1.12 h
1.13 k
1.14 n

REFLECT

1.15 i
1.16 f
1.17 m
1.18 j
1.19 l
1.20 h
1.21 c
1.22 k
1.23 a
1.24 b
1.25 g
1.26 d
1.27 e

RECITE

1.28 different
1.29 culture
1.30 communicate
1.31 society
1.32 behavior
1.33 labeling
1.34 normal
1.35 special
1.36 handicapped
1.37 environment
1.38 deviance
1.39 others
1.40 differences
1.41 education
1.42 setting
1.43 conditions

REVIEW

1.44 c
1.45 d
1.46 a
1.47 c
1.48 c
1.49 a
1.50 c
1.51 a
1.52 c
1.53 a
1.54 a
1.55 c
1.56 d
1.57 d
1.58 b
1.59 b
1.60 b
1.61 b
1.62 c
1.63 b
1.64 a
1.65 b
1.66 d
1.67 c
1.68 d
1.69 c
1.70 d
1.71 a

Chapter Two

Multicultural and Diversity Issues

Preview

This chapter compares the basic purposes of general education with the underlying purposes of multicultural and special education, noting effects on the public schools of recent significant increases in the numbers of culturally diverse students. The role of traditional assessment procedures in the over-representation of culturally different children in special education is considered, including aspects of cultural bias in the nature and administration of the tests. The authors explain ways in which differing cultural-social mores influence the nature and degree of parent involvement in the education process. In considering the development of the IEP, those areas that require particular attention when providing services in the least restrictive environment for a culturally different student are discussed. Poverty and migrancy are discussed as factors contributing to the academic difficulties often experienced by these students. The chapter concludes with a discussion of the stigma often associated with special education. The phenomenon of self-fulfilling prophesy is addressed, as well as the importance of individualizing a students' instruction.

Question

Try to answer these questions during your first reading of the chapter.

In what three ways do the purposes and approaches to general education sometimes differ from those of special and multicultural education?

Can you describe the population status and trends of culturally diverse groups, including their impact on the U. S. educational system?

In what two ways may assessment contribute to overrepresentation of students who are culturally diverse in special education programs?

Can you name three ways language diversity may contribute to inaccurate assessment of culturally diverse children?

In what three ways may differing cultural-social mores affect parent involvement in education?

What two areas require particular attention when developing an IEP for a student who is culturally different?

Why is it difficult to provide the "least restrictive environment" for students who are culturally different?

In what two ways may poverty contribute to the academic difficulties of students who are culturally different, possibly resulting in their referral to special education?

In what two ways may migrancy contribute to academic difficulties of students who are culturally diverse?

What three conceptual factors have contributed to increased attention and concern over placing ethnically and culturally diverse students in special education?

Read

Match these terms found in Chapter Two with their meanings.

a. multicultural education
b. cultural pluralism
c. prevalence
d. melting pot
e. test bias
f. negative stigma
g. overrepresentation
h. measurement bias

2.1 ______ A situation in which many cultures are blended into one.
2.2 ______ The unfairness of a testing procedure or instrument which gives one group an advantage or another group a disadvantage.
2.3 ______ The number of people in a given population who exhibit a condition, problem, or particular status.
2.4 ______ Many cultural subgroups living together in a manner that maintains cultural differences.
2.5 ______ Education that promotes learning about multiple cultures and values.
2.6 ______ A situation in which one cultural group has a higher percentage of youngsters in special education than might be expected.
2.7 ______ An unflattering view of someone associated with the label given to that person.
2.8 ______ Unfairness or inaccuracy of assessment due to cultural background, sex, or race.

Reflect

Match each term with its correct meaning.

a. norm-based averages
b. U.S. general education
c. special education
d. self-fulfilling prophecy
e. acculturation process
f. impoverished environment
g. assessment tools
h. nondiscriminatory assessment

2.9 _______ Institution that provides an education for the masses.
2.10 _______ Field in which the basic purpose is dealing with differences.
2.11 _______ Prediction that an individual will become what he or she is labeled.
2.12 _______ The instruments, or tests, used to evaluate students.
2.13 _______ Testing that does not result in inaccurate reflections of ability.
2.14 _______ The average performance scores of agemates.
2.15 _______ Home/neighborhood or community lacking important resources.
2.16 _______ Socialization resulting from one's unique social/cultural environment.

Recite

Complete each sentence with a term that best expresses the meaning. Try to get all eight correct without referring to the chapter.

2.17 A major purpose of general education is to provide education for the masses and to bring all students to a similar level of ___________.

2.18 Current special education efforts focus on individual ______________.

2.19 Effective educational programming for culturally diverse students requires a _______ effort.

2.20 There is a negative stigma related to _________.

2.21 Special education services for students who are from cultural minority groups may not be educationally effective in meeting their ___________ problems.

2.22 Children who do not speak English may be viewed by some educators as having speech or language ________.

2.23 Not speaking a society's dominant _________________ may result in an inaccurate assessment of a child's academic abilities.

2.24 In many cases, economic disadvantage and language differences are found in situations of____________.

Review

This exercise will help you at test time! Choose the best of four possible answers.

2.25 Which statement represents the purpose of multicultural education?
- a. It is intended to teach all students about cultural diversity.
- b. It is intended to be limited to those of cultural or racial minorities.
- c. It is intended to exist apart from general education.
- d. It is intended to promote special education programs for minority students.

2.26 Multicultural education was introduced as a result of
- a. societal unrest due to poverty and economic recession
- b. the realization that culturally diverse students learn better when segregated for academics
- c. the perception that needs of students with cultural differences were not being met
- d. the emergence of federal funding to support the NCA

2.27 A major purpose of general education is to
- a. prepare students for college
- b. presumably provide education for everyone
- c. promote individual differences
- d. keep teenagers off the street

2.28 One way that assessment has contributed to potential overrepresentation of culturally different students in special education is through assessment instruments that were designed and constructed with specific language content favoring
- a. the cultural majority
- b. the cultural minority
- c. the wealthy population
- d. the migrant population

2.29 Multicultural education advocates contend that mislabeling has led to over-representation of culturally different children in special education, primarily because of

a. the self-fulfilling prophecy
b. ineffective special education programs
c. incompetent school administrators and teachers
d. discrimination by the cultural majority

2.30 Which of these statements about prevalence figures is true?

a. A high percentage of special education students are from culturally divergent backgrounds.
b. There is no difference in drop-out rates for minority and majority youngsters.
c. Students from culturally divergent backgrounds are equally represented with majority students in gifted and talented programs.
d. Drop-out rates are not associated with level of income.

2.31 Concern has been expressed that special education for cultural minority students has been used to

a. teach English to non-English speaking youngsters
b. prepare minority students for menial level jobs
c. remediate learning deficits that are not there
d. separate racial minorities from majority

2.32 Multicultural education is viewed as education that values and promotes

a. individualism
b. homogeneity
c. cultural separatism
d. cultural pluralism

2.33 An impoverished environment may affect children because of

a. inadequate nutrition
b. lack of TV
c. little language diversity
d. genotypic deficiency

2.34 Moving from city to city may adversely affect a child's

a. relationship with other children
b. academic progress
c. ability to obtain needed services
d. all of the above

2.35 Probably the most important preparation for teachers and other professionals responsible for delivering multicultural education to culturally diverse students is

a. fluency in a language other than English
b. general knowledge of and sensitivity to various cultures
c. ability to conceal prejudices
d. knowledge of fundamental principles of psychology and sociology

2.36 Certain behaviors that may suggest a disabling condition that needs special education assistance may be viewed as normal in some

a. cultural environments
b. school environments
c. social environments
d. home environments

2.37 Minority groups who support multicultural education believe that

a. special education is the best placement for most students
b. placement in special education may promote a negative stigma
c. students should only be educated in their native tongue
d. students from culturally diverse backgrounds shouldn't have to attend school with the majority

2.38 The primary focus of an IEP for a student from a culturally different background should be

a. individual needs of the child
b. language instruction
c. decreasing culturally diversity
d. academic skills

2.39 Many parents are reluctant to have their child receive special help because

a. it interferes with extra-curricular activities
b. they feel a negative stigma is attached
c. they feel their child should be able to achieve in school without help
d. they do not understand what special education is

ANSWER KEY FOR CHAPTER TWO

READ

2.1 d
2.2 e
2.3. c
2.4. b
2.5. a
2.6. g
2.7. f
2.8. h

RECITE

2.9 performance
2.10 needs, strengths
2.11 team
2.12 special education
2.13 academic
2.14 disorders
2.15 language
2.16 migrancy

REFLECT

2.17 b
2.18 c
2.19 d
2.20 g
2.21 h
2.22 a
2.23 f
2.24 e

REVIEW

2.25 a
2.26 c
2.27 b
2.28 a
2.29 d
2.30 a
2.31 d
2.32 d
2.33 a
2.34 d
2.35 b
2.36 a
2.37 b
2.38 a
2.39 b

Chapter Three

Exceptionality and the Family

Preview

The birth of a baby with a significant disability can deeply impact a family in a number of ways. This chapter describes the effects on family members and professionals who deal with exceptionalities, based on a social/ecological system approach. Many parents and family issues are discussed, including individual emotional stability, religious values, cultural beliefs, and family socioeconomic status, as impacted by the severity and type of the child's disability.

Mothers and fathers of children with disabilities may be affected in diverse ways. The range and sequence of emotions can be highly variable, with some parents moving through distinct phases and stages and others being more recursive in their feelings. Four common reactions of parents are described: shock, realization, defensive retreat, and acknowledgment.

Parenting children with disabilities can cause strain in marital, parent-child, and sibling relationships. Problems can also arise within the extended family.

The interaction that occurs between professionals and parents may be marked with confusion and anger. Chapter Three concludes with information about training programs for parents, professionals, and family members. Collaboration between parents and professionals may improve the overall likelihood and quality of success that students and teachers experience in achieving academic, social, and life-long goals.

Question

After previewing Chapter Three you should be able to respond successfully to the following questions:

What five factors influence the ways in which a family may respond to an infant with a birth defect or disability?

What three things are known about the stages that parents may experience in responding to an infant or young child with a disability?

In what three ways may a newborn child with a disability influence the family social system?

What three factors involved with raising a child with a disability may contribute to marital stress?

The four general phases of the developmental cycle parents typically go through in raising a child with a disability include?

What four factors influence the relationship that develops between an infant with a disability and his or her mother?

In what three ways may a father respond to his child with a disability?

Can you name four ways in which siblings respond to a brother or sister with a disability?

What three types of assistance can grandparents give to a family with a child with a disability?

The three types of professional understanding are essential to establishing positive relationships with parents and families of children with disabilities are?

What are five goals of family support systems?

Can you describe the five goals of parent training?

Read

These are terms you need to know from Chapter Three. Match them with their correct meanings. Get all nine and you're doing fine!

a. shock
b. realization
c. defensive retreat
d. acknowledgment
e. dyadic relationship
f. marital stress
g. extended family
h. social/ecological systems approach
i. family empowerment

3.1 ________ Phase at which parents are able to mobilize their strengths to confront the conditions created by having an exceptional child.

3.2 ________ Phase at which parents attempt to avoid dealing with the anxiety-producing realities of their child's exceptionality.

3.3 ________ Phase at which parents may be anxious or fearful about their ability to cope with the demands of caring for a child with unique needs.

3.4 ________ A stage that may be distinguished by feelings of anxiety, guilt, numbness, confusion, and/or helplessness.

3.5 ________ Attachment that occurs between two people, particularly strong on occasion between a mother and her child with a disability.

3.6 _______ Pressure in a relationship between husband and wife.

3.7 _______ People who are close relatives and have regular and frequent contact with the family.

3.8 _______ Enabling families to effectively meet both their needs and the child's needs.

3.9 _______ A theory that describes the interrelationships among family members and the effects family members have on one another.

Reflect

Here are more items for you to correctly identify.

a. spina bifida and Down syndrome
b. hearing impairments and learning disabilities
c. shock
d. Kids as Self-Advocates (KASA)
e. mother-child relationship
f. father-child relationship
g. parent training
h. emotional disorganization
i. developmental cycle
j. respite care programs

3.10 ______ Relationship in which expectations and functions in nurturing play a significant role.

3.11 ______ Relationship that often develops differently depending on the exceptional child's gender.

3.12 ______ Club providing opportunities for youth with disabilities and their friends to develop leadership skills.

3.13 ______ Examples of conditions that are readily apparent at birth.

3.14 ______ Examples of conditions that are not evident until later in life.

3.15 ______ Condition in which parents may be unable to process information presented by professionals.

3.16 ______ Intervention that helps parents develop appropriate expectations for their child's current and future achievement.

3.17 ______ A period when parents question the meaning of life and the reasons for their present challenges.

3.18 ______ Temporary care for disabled children so that parents have an opportunity to relax and renew their relationship.

3.19 ______ General phases that parents go through in raising an exceptional child.

Recite

This is a good check on what you have learned in Chapter Three. Complete each of the eight items.

3.20 A major concern of parents of an exceptional child is what their child will be capable of as an _____.

3.21 A mother and her child with a disability develop a _____________ relationship.

3.22 Factors such as reduction of time available for couple activities, financial burdens, and fatigue can cause ____________ stress.

3.23 The first phase of the developmental cycle that parents undergo in raising an exceptional child is the period_____________.

3.24 There is a significant correlation between grandparent support and positive _________ adjustment.

3.25 The third phase of the developmental cycle is the ____________period.

3.26 The fourth phase of the developmental cycle is the period when the parents are no longer able to provide direct care and _________________ for their son or daughter.

3.27 Grandparents of a child with a disability can provide child's parents with a reprieve from the pressures of the ______________ environment.

Review

Choose the best of the four possible answers listed. This exercise should help you test your understanding of Chapter Three.

3.28 Which factor most strongly influences the ways in which family members respond to an infant with a birth defect or disability?
a. Employment status of father
b. The parents' occupations
c. The severity of the disability
d. The number of siblings in the family

3.29 Which statement is most accurate regarding the four stages that parents go through in accepting an exceptionality in an infant or young child (shock, realization, defensive retreat, acknowledgment)?
a. The stages are generally the same among parents.
b. Shock lasts the longest of the stages.
c. The mother reaches acknowledgment first.
d. The process of adjustment for parents is continuous and distinctly individual.

3.30 Which of the following does Chapter Three mention as a major concern of parents of an exceptional child?
a. What the child will be capable of as an adult
b. How to conceal their child's disability
c. What psychiatric services the child will need
d. Who is responsible for the disability

3.31 Typically what is the immediate reaction of parents to learning that an infant has a disability?
a. Shock
b. Anger
c. Fear
d. Rejection

3.32 Essential components of family-centered support include:
a. addressing family needs holistically
b. normalizing perspectives
c. considering family strengths
d. all of the above

3.33 The fourth phase of the developmental cycle is the period when parents
a. must care for most needs of their child with a disability
b. enter their child with a disability into a residential setting
c. are no longer able to provide direct care and guidance for their child with a disability
d. reject special education in favor of home-based education

3.34 The first phase of the developmental cycle, when the parents try to determine if the child has a disability, is called the
a. identification period
b. screening phase
c. diagnostic period
d. acknowledgment phase

3.35 Which does Chapter Three describe as a way in which a sibling is likely to react to an exceptional child?
  a. Run away from home
  b. Respond differently than the parents
  c. Respond the same way as the parents
  d. Never accept the exceptional child

3.36 Which does Chapter Three describe as a way in which a father may react to his exceptional child?
  a. He will blame his wife.
  b. He is likely to externalize his feelings.
  c. He will respond the same way to either a son or a daughter with a disability.
  d. He may resent time spent by his wife in caring for their exceptional child.

3.37 An organization designed to help siblings of exceptional children is
  a. the Sibling Information Network
  b. the Organization of Siblings of the Disabled (OSD)
  c. the Association of Siblings of the Disabled
  d. the American Sibling Association (ASA)

3.38 Which of the following is recommended by Chapter Three as a way that grandparents can give assistance to families with a child with a disability?
  a. Providing educational toys
  b. Babysitting
  c. Visiting only at pre-arranged times
  d. Accepting some of the blame

3.39 At what stage are parents best able to receive and comprehend nformation concerning their child who has a disability?
  a. Shock stage
  b. Defensive retreat stage
  c. Realization stage
  d. Acknowledgment stage

3.40 Research related to marital stress and instability of parents who have a child with a disability
  a. is limited and contradictory
  b. reveals an increased incidence of divorce
  c. suggests that some couples report improvements in their marital relationship
  d. indicates that these parents have no more marital problems that other families with children

3.41 Research has indicated that grandparents play a particularly influential role during the ___________________ in helping their own children respond appropriately to having a child with a disability.

a. intervention planning phase
b. diagnostic phase
c. initial treatment phase
d. placement phase

3.42 Services for young children with disabilities are now primarily directed at

a. the family as a whole
b. the parents and child with the disability
c. the siblings and the child with the disability
d. the parents and grandparents who live nearby

3.43 Recent research suggests that family support services have

a. substantially increased local and state government expenditures for caring for children and youth with disabilities
b. substantially decreased out-of-home placements of children with disabilities
c. substantially increased educational and social achievement in children with disabilities
d. decreased hospitalization of children and youth with disabilities

3.44 Training for professionals with regard to families focuses primarily on

a. negotiation, assertiveness, and communication skills
b. relationship building, communication, and collaboration skills
c. problem solving, delegation, and negotiation skills
d. intervention, problem solving, and assertiveness skills

ANSWER KEY FOR CHAPTER THREE

READ

3.1 d
3.2 c
3.3 b
3.4 a
3.5 e
3.6 f
3.7 g
3.8 i
3.9 h

REFLECT

3.10 e
3.11 f
3.12 d
3.13 a
3.14 b
3.15 c
3.16 g
3.17 h
3.18 j
3.19 i

RECITE

3.20 adult
3.21 dyadic
3.22 marital
3.23 diagnostic
3.24 paternal
3.25 post-public school
3.26 guidance
3.27 home

REVIEW

3.28 c
3.29 d
3.30 a
3.31 a
3.32 c
3.33 c
3.34 c
3.35 c
3.36 d
3.37 a
3.38 b
3.39 d
3.40 a
3.41 b
3.42 a
3.43 b
3.44 b

Chapter Four

The Early Childhood and Elementary School Years: Special Education, Inclusion, and Collaboration

Preview

This chapter describes education and other services for young children with disabilities, from infancy through the transition into the early years of elementary school. The authors provide a brief historical review of early intervention, an explanation of its current definition, a discussion of the rationale for such services, and a description of service delivery options that are available.

The chapter also describes the early elementary school years, including the roles and responsibilities of the consulting teacher, the resource-room teacher and teacher-assistance or school wide teams. Characteristics of effective inclusive schools, and other educational settings, are discussed. The authors explain three characteristics of special education – individualization, intensive instruction and explicit teaching. The four phrase special education referral, planning, and placement process is also described.

The chapter concludes by describing two models of collaboration and identifying three types of peer support programs. This chapter, along with chapter 5, will give you a foundation for understanding chapters 6-17, which are concerned with specific types of exceptionality.

Question

While studying the material on early childhood and elementary school years, you should find answers to these questions:

Why is it so important to provide early intervention services as soon as possible for young children at risk?

What are the essential components in the Individualized Family Service Plan?

What are the critical services and programs for pre-school age children?

What three characteristics of special education enhance learning opportunities for students with disabilities?

What is meant by *adaptive fit* and *adaptive instruction* for students with disabilities?

What four steps are necessary to refer a child for special education services?

What are the characteristics of effective inclusive schools and classrooms?

How is collaboration defined, and what are the differences between a consulting teacher, a resource room teacher, and teacher assistance teams?

What is the general educator's role in meeting the needs of students with disabilities?

What is the difference between peer and cross-age tutoring versus cooperative learning?

What types of special education classrooms and/or schools are available for students with disabilities?

What are the pros and cons of full inclusion for students with disabilities?

Read

These are important terms from Chapter Four that you should know. Matching them correctly shows that you understand key points.

a. Individualized Family Service Plan (IFSP)
b. the "adaptive fit"
c. service coordination
d. consulting teacher
e. resource room
f. "pull-out"
g. authentic assessment
h. self-contained special education classroom
i. special school
j. basic-skills approach
k. intensity
l. functional life skills
m. home school
n. interactive teaming
o. intensive-care specialists
p. full inclusion
q. cooperative learning
r. peer & cross-age tutoring
s. peer-mediated instruction
t. mainstreaming

4.1 ________The school students would attend were they not exceptional.

4.2 ________ Instruction that focuses on skills that will facilitate the student's accommodation to society.

4.3 ________ An arrangement in which school staff engage in reciprocal efforts to meet a common goal.

4.4 ________ Compatibility between demands of the educational setting and abilities of the student.

4.5 ________ Coordination of various services provided to the child with a disability and/or the family.

4.6 ________ An intervention plan for infants and pre-school children and their families.

4.7 ________ Placement for students who require intensive and specialized education services.

4.8 ________ An individual who supports general classroom teachers.

4.9 ________ A program that removes a student with a disability from the general classroom to a resource room for part of the school day.

4.10 ________ A program that provides individualized instruction to students who attend general education programs.

4.11 ________ Curriculum that teaches a specified set of skills in a sequential order.

4.12 ________ A system that provides educational services in a separate facility for students with disabilities.

4.13 ________ The frequency and amount of time a young child is engaged in intervention activities.

4.14 ________ A variety of performance based assessments requiring responses in a real-life context.

4.15 ________ Those working in Neonatal Intensive Care Units (NICU's) with babies who have special needs.

4.16 ________ A system which places students with disabilities in general education classrooms for some classes.

4.17 ________ Use of classmates to reinforce the teacher's instruction.

4.18 ________ Classroom procedures that emphasize individual learning.

4.19 ________ Strategies that emphasize simultaneous/group learning.

4.20 ________ Model using a partnership of general and special educators providing services in the general education classrooms in the student's home school.

Reflect

Below are additional terms that represent other important points from Ch. 4. Match them with appropriate definitions.

a. early intervention
b. adaptive fit
c. early childhood special education
d. adaptive instruction

e. collaboration
f. Handicapped Children's Early Education Program
g. functional assessment
h. consulting teacher
i. resource-room teacher
j. TAT or SWAT
k. child-find
l. at-risk condition
m. individualization
n. Head Start
o. intensive instruction

4.21________ Groups of professionals, students, and/or parents working together to solve problems and support classroom.
4.22________ The first program that focused on plans and methodologies to meet the needs of young children with disabilities.
4.23________ Determination of a child's skills, the characteristics of the setting, as well as the family's needs, resources, and expectations.
4.24________ System in each state set up to identify young children who are at risk and make referrals to the local education agency.
4.25________ Developmental delay that may result in a disability.
4.26________ Preventive steps taken early in life to lessen the impact of a disability.
4.27________ Comprehensive intervention services for at-risk or disabled infants and children.
4.28________ A student's ability to cope with the requirements of a school setting.
4.29________ Adaptation of learning environments to accommodate the unique needs of individual students.
4.30________ One or more people working together to attain a common goal.
4.31________ Professionals with advanced training who have knowledge of various instructional strategies.
4.32________ Professionals who provide individualized instruction outside the regular classroom.
4.33________ A student-centered approach to instructional decision making.
4.34________ Program providing early enrichment experiences.
4.35________ Frequent instructional experiences of significant duration.

Recite

Supply words from Chapter Four that best complete each statement.

4.36 The first years of life are crucial to the overall development of children who are normal, at-risk, and ______________.

4.37 Early ____________ has a significant impact on later development of language, intelligence, personality, and sense of worth.

4.38 Intervention should begin as early as possible in an environment which is free of traditional disability ____________.

4.39 Early intervention has the potential to lessen the overall impact of ____________.

4.40 Early childhood special education is the process of carefully responding to a well-conceived __________ education/treatment plan.

4.41 Early intervention services must be provided throughout the early years without significant periods of ___________.

4.42 The ability of a child to cope with the demands of the educational environment depends upon the type and ____________ of the disability.

<u>**Review**</u>

Try to answer these questions without referring back to the chapter. Completing this exercise independently is a good way to find out how well you comprehend what you have just read.

4.43 Which is the earliest piece of legislation regarding early childhood services for young children?

a. Public Law 94-142
b. Children's Early Assistance Act
c. Public Law 98-199
d. Public Law 99-457

4.44 Why is early intervention critical for infants and children with disabilities or at-risk conditions?

a. To lessen the long-term impact of a disability
b. To provide the young child with intensive medical care
c. To prevent the family from participating in the intervention process
d. To place the child in a specific category for special education services as early as possible

4.45 Major goals of early childhood special education include
a. lessening the impact of conditions that may worsen without timely treatment
b. providing specialized therapies
c. providing children with the pre-academic skills necessary for further learning
d. all of the above

4.46 Another term for the basic-skills approach is the
a. functional approach
b. remedial approach
c. developmental approach
d. life approach

4.47 What is meant by "adaptive fitting" for students with disabilities?
a. A program for students with severe behavior disorders
b. The degree to which an individual is able to cope with the requirements of the school setting
c. A child with a disability who is unable to adapt to the regular classroom environment
d. The degree to which the regular classroom teacher can assist students with disabilities

4.48 A major breakthrough in the education of students with disabilities is the emergence of
a. specialized services available in self-contained special education classrooms
b. classroom teachers who specialize in school subjects
c. collaborative efforts between classroom teachers and the specialists available within the public schools
d. separate programs, special schools, and more specialized services

4.49 Which educational model offers support to classroom teachers through professionals or specialists emphasizing modification of the regular classroom environment to accommodate exceptional students?
a. The resource room model
b. The consulting teacher model
c. The special school model
d. The self-contained special education classroom model

4.50 Which approach has been predominantly used to instruct students with disabilities?
a. The resource room model
b. The consulting teacher model
c. The self-contained special education classroom model
d. The special school model

4.51 The self-contained special education classroom

a. employs an itinerant teacher to recommend intervention strategies to regular classroom teachers
b. employs a special education teacher who provides individualized instruction for short periods during the school day
c. is considered the least restrictive environment for most students with learning/behavior disorders
d. employs the expertise of a qualified special education teacher to work with students who require specialized instruction for the majority of the day

4.52 Which curricular approach teaches content areas while emphasizing daily living skills, personal-social competencies, communication abilities, vocational skills, and other practical competencies?

a. Remediation of academic deficits
b. Systematic instruction of academic subject areas
c. Functional life skills
d. Basic academic skills

4.53 Which curricular emphasis is typical for children with disabilities during the elementary school years?

a. Academic and socialization
b. Occupational/vocational
c. Recreational/leisure
d. Pre-academic and socialization

4.54 Early intervention delivery models include

a. home-based programs
b. school-based programs
c. a combination of home and school-based programs
d. all of the above

4.55 Current Head Start programs

a. have no provisions for the education of students with disabilities
b. are primarily for the purpose of funding school lunch programs for preschool-age children who are disadvantaged
c. require that at least 10% of their enrollment be reserved for children with disabilities
d. have enrollments of about 50% children from disadvantaged backgrounds and 50% children with disabilities

4.56 Effective inclusive schools are characterized by
a. special education personnel consistently placed in the role of expert
b. general educators with sole responsibility for students with disabilities
c. services and support provided to all students in age-appropriate classrooms
d. competitive relationships between general and special education personnel

4.57 Cooperative learning has been successful primarily in
a. teaching academic skills
b. teaching social interaction skills
c. creating learning opportunities for students with and without disabilities
d. all of the above

4.58 Collaboration is characterized by
a. the special education teacher having primary responsibility for students with disabilities, with support from the general education teacher
b. the general education teacher having primary responsibility for students with disabilities, with support from the special educator
c. general and special educators working independently of each other to support the student in achieving a common goal
d. co-equal interaction between general and special educators who are working as partners to achieve a common goal

4.59 A resource room program can best be described as
a. a study hall area for students to complete difficult homework assignments
b. a program for students to receive specialized instruction to support and supplement their work in the general education settting
c. a special education classroom in which students spend the majority of their school day
d. a classroom supervised by a general education classroom teacher with in-class support from a special educator

4.60 General education teachers identified which of the following as a problem with inclusion:
a. lack of instruction regarding appropriate instructional adaptations
b. disruptive students who lacked the necessary social and behavioral skills
c. lack of specialized assistance from a special education teacher
d. all of the above

4.61 Supporters of full inclusion would advocate placement in a

a. general education class with pull-out into a resource room or part-time special education class
b. self-contained special education classroom with some opportunities for interactions with non-disabled students
c. a general education classroom with in-class support for students with disabilities
d. all of the above

ANSWER KEY FOR CHAPTER FOUR

READ

4.1 m
4.2 l
4.3 n
4.4 b
4.5 c
4.6 a
4.7 h
4.8 d
4.9 f
4.10 e
4.11 j
4.12 i
4.13 k
4.14 g
4.15 o
4.16 t
4.17 s
4.18 r
4.19 q
4.20 p

REFLECT

4.21 j
4.22 f
4.23 g
4.24 k
4.25 l
4.26 a
4.27 c
4.28 b
4.29 d
4.30 e
4.31 h
4.32 i
4.33 m
4.34 n
4.35 o

RECITE

4.36 disabled
4.37 stimulation
4.38 labels
4.39 disabilities
4.40 individual
4.41 interruption
4.42 severity

REVIEW

4.43 d
4.44 a
4.45 d
4.46 c
4.47 b
4.48 c
4.49 b
4.50 a
4.51 d
4.52 c
4.53 a
4.54 d
4.55 c
4.56 c
4.57 d
4.58 d
4.59 b
4.60 d
4.61 c

Chapter Five

Transition From School and the Adult Years

Preview

This chapter focuses on the instruction and services secondary schools provide for youth with disabilities and on the continuing needs of adults with disabilities. Transition planning and services are described, and the legal requirements for transition services are described.

The Individualized Transition Plan (ITP) is defined, and the importance of involving students and parents as well as adult service agencies is addressed. Implementing transition services in secondary schools is described. The major curriculum areas are covered, including self-determination, academic skills, adaptive and functional life skills, and employment preparation.

Issues associated with the adult years are also addressed: making choices, building a support network, using government funded programs, and natural supports. Issues for aging adults with disabilities are also discussed.

Question

While previewing this chapter, be prepared to find answers to these questions:

What three reasons are given for planning the transition of students with disabilities from school to adult life?

How does IDEA define transition services?

What should be included in each student's IEP statement regarding transition services and who should be involved in the planning process?

What three outcomes are expected for adolescents with disabilities as they enter adulthood?

Why is it important for secondary students with disabilities to receive instruction in self-determination, academics, adaptive and functional skills, and employment preparation?

What are the purposes of government-supported programs for people with disabilities in the areas of income support, health care, residential living, and employment?

What two challenges are faced by aging people with disabilities?

Read

These terms from Chapter Five are important for you to understand. Match them with their meanings.

a. transition services
b. Vocational Rehabilitation Act
c. Carl Perkins Act
d. functional academic programs
e. community-referenced instruction
f. Work Incentives Act of 1999
g. Medicaid
h. vocational rehabilitation

5.1 ______ Legislation enabling people with disabilities to work and keep health care coverage.
5.2 ______ A federal mandate providing services for adults with disabilities through rehabilitation counselors in several areas.
5.3 ______ Curriculum that concentrates on providing information and protection to high school students with disabilities.
5.4 ______ A coordinated set of student activities that promote movement from school to post-school activities.
5.5 ______ Legislation providing students with disabilities greater access to vocational education services.
5.6 ______ A program involving direct training and ongoing support in a community employment site.
5.7 ______ A program providing intensive, short-term support to people with disabilities who can undertake successful employment on their own.
5.8 ______ A government-sponsored health care program for people with disabilities.

Reflect

These terms relate to high school and transition to adult life.

a. transition
b. School to Work Act
c. exploratory curriculum
d. self-determination
e. work experience program
f. adult service agencies

g. entitlement program

5.9 ______ Program in which a student spends a portion of the school day at an off-campus site receiving on-the-job training.

5.10 ______ Experiences providing a direct link between the concepts/skills learned in elementary school and knowledge gained in high school.

5.11 ______ The ability of a person to consider options and to make appropriate choices regarding residential life, work and leisure time.

5.12 ______ A term defined by Will (1984) as a "bridge between the security and structure offered by the school and adult life."

5.13 ______ Legislation providing all students in the public schools with education and training to prepare them for first jobs.

5.14 ______ A type of government adult service program for people with disabilities wherein anyone eligible must receive the service.

5.15 ______ Agencies providing services to adults with disabilities, accessing postsecondary education, participating in leisure activities, etc.

Recite

Fill in the blanks with words that complete the meaning of the sentences.

5.16 One crucial issue facing students with disabilities, their parents, and educators is the _________ between school instruction and eventual adult needs.

5.17 According to U.S. Dept. of Education (2000) data, only _______ % of students with disabilities leave high school with a diploma.

5.18 Without question, the ____________ of adults with disabilities has been significantly underestimated.

5.19 Nearly ____________ a million students with disabilities exit school each year.

5.20 Students with disabilities are not doing well in the _______ content of high school or in further postsecondary education.

5.21 The failure of people with disabilities in the workplace has been linked to a lack of appropriate ____________ ____________ skills.

5.22 For students with disabilities, high schools have been somewhat __________ in their approach to employment preparation.

5.23 Many students with disabilities and their parents receive a considerable _____________ during the transition from high school to the adult world.

5.24 Adults with disabilities are significantly _______________ and underemployed when compared to their nondisabled peers.

5.25 Life expectancy for all adults, including those with _____________ continues to increase.

Review

This is good practice for an exam on material from Chapter Five.

5.26 A study found that employment following school for people with disabilities was directly linked to

a. successful completion of high school graduation requirements
b. severity of the student's disability
c. opportunities for students to work while still in school
d. the availability of vocational education and rehabilitation counseling services

5.27 Many of the current graduates from special education programs are

a. not adequately prepared for employment following school
b. not adequately prepared for postsecondary education
c. unable to access programs and services necessary for success during adulthood
d. all of the above

5.28 The transition planning process for students with disabilities should begin

a. during the year the student is expected to graduate (ages 18-21)
b. at age 14 and not later than age 16
c. immediately following graduation from high school
d. as soon as the multidisciplinary team determines that the student is ready for a job

5.29 The principal components of a transition planning system include

a. effective high school instruction
b. a cooperative system of transition planning
c. interagency coordination
d. all of the above

5.30 The primary route to postsecondary education for students with disabilities is
a. vocational rehabilitation counseling
b. the natural support system of the family
c. vocational education and academic programs
d. a transition planning process that begins immediately following graduation from high school

5.31 Available research indicates that students with disabilities are
a. doing as well as can be expected in the academic content of high school programs
b. doing as well as can be expected in postsecondary education
c. dropping out of high school at a high rate
d. all of the above

5.32 Concerning high school programs for students with mild disabilities, Zigmond suggests that schools have *more* intense instruction in
a. career planning
b. functional skills
c. reading and mathematics
d. vocational training

5.33 For students with severe disabilities, academic learning during the secondary school years should be more
a. protection oriented
b. functional and compensatory
c. leisure time oriented
d. content focused (reading and mathematics)

5.34 Research indicates that individuals with disabilities fail on the job most often because
a. they lack decision making skills
b. they can't do the required tasks
c. they lack transportation to and from work
d. all of the above

5.35 "Direct training and ongoing support as necessary in a community employment site" is a description of
a. community-referenced instruction
b. career education
c. work activity centers
d. work experience

5.36 The purpose of an individualized transition plan is to
a. identify the range of services an individual needs to participate in the community
b. identify activities that must occur during the high school years
c. establish timelines and responsibilities for completion of these activities
d. all of the above

5.37 During the transition from school to adult life, students and parents may realize that
a. individuals are entitled to services during adulthood as well as during school years
b. a person with a disability has little difficulty accessing needed supports and services during adult years
c. they have little knowledge regarding how the adult service system works
d. all of the above

5.38 For most of the twentieth century, federal support for residential living has been directed toward
a. families
b. small group homes
c. large congregate care living
d. all of the above

5.39 A residential model for people with disabilities who may require minimal on-going supervision and support is
a. nursing homes
b. group homes
c. foster family care
d. semi-independent apartments or homes

5.40 Provision of time-limited support services for people with disabilities is most often associated with
a. supported employment
b. sheltered workshops
c. vocational rehabilitation
d. work activity centers

5.41 Criteria for placement in supported employment include

a. full-time (40 hours/week) employment
b. hourly rate not to exceed minimum wage
c. fringe benefits similar to those provided for nondisabled workers
d. all of the above

5.42 The zero-exclusion principle is most closely associated with which of the following employment services

a. vocational rehabilitation
b. supported employment
c. sheltered workshops
d. work experience

5.43 Research on community living options for aging people with disabilities indicates

a. a trend toward smaller community living options
b. a trend toward larger congregate care living
c. no change in living options in recent years
d. an increase in both smaller and larger community living options

5.44 According to Heller (2000), there are about

a. 20% of the adult population who have a disability
b. half a million adults with developmental disabilities 60 or older
c. half the adult population in the U.S. with a disability
d. 20 % of the population with disabilities living to age 75

ANSWER KEY FOR CHAPTER FIVE

READ
5.1 f
5.2 b
5.3 d
5.4 a
5.5 c
5.6 e
5.7 h
5.8 g

REFLECT
5.9 e
5.10 c
5.11 d
5.12 a
5.13 b
5.14 g
5.15 f

RECITE
5.16 relationship
5.17 25%
5.18 potential
5.19 half
5.20 academic
5.21 decision making
5.22 passive
5.23 shock
5.24 unemployed
5.25 disabilities

REVIEW
5.26 c
5.27 d
5.28 b
5.29 d
5.30 c
5.31 c
5.32 c
5.33 b
5.34 a
5.35 a
5.36 d
5.37 c
5.38 c
5.39 d
5.40 c
5.41 c
5.42 b
5.43 a
5.44 b

Chapter Six

People with Learning Disabilities

Preview

The category of learning disabilities has generated more controversy, confusion, and polarization among professionals than any other area of exceptionality. The term *learning disabilities* is a generic educational label that includes a variety of different conditions causing academic behavioral as well as performance deficits. This chapter presents four reasons why definitions associated with learning disabilities are varied and imprecise.

The authors explain that typically children with learning disabilities have normal intelligence, but they experience academic difficulties and often social problems as well. Although estimates of prevalence vary for all types of exceptionality, the area of learning disabilities generates the widest discrepancy, as well as being the largest and most varied category of disability served in the public schools.

Chapter Six outlines characteristics of children with discrepancies and disabilities in the following areas: (1) academic achievement, (2) intelligence, (3) cognition and information processing, (4) learning characteristics, (5) hyperactivity, and (6) social and emotional characteristics. Although causes of learning disabilities are difficult to discern, professional efforts to examine neurological factors, maturational delay, genetic factors, and environmental factors are explored.

Assessment procedures are employed to appropriately screen, identify, and determine placement for individuals who require special services. The authors examine assessment issues in terms of purpose and domain of assessment, focusing on intelligence, adaptive skills, and academic achievement.

Intervention strategies for children and adolescents are discussed under the categories of academic and behavioral. Transition to adult life, and inclusive education for students with LD are then addressed. The chapter concludes with a discussion of medical services available during childhood and adolescence for students with learning disabilities.

Question

After studying Chapter Six you should be able to provide answers to the questions below:

What are four reasons for the wide variation in the definitions of learning disabilities?

In what two ways can people with learning disabilities be classified?

What two estimate ranges are given for the prevalence of learning disabilities?

What seven characteristics are generally attributed to people with learning disabilities, and why it is difficult to characterize this group?

What four causes are thought to be involved in learning disabilities?

What four questions are addressed in screening assessment for learning disabilities?

What three types of intervention or treatment are employed with children diagnosed as having learning disabilities?

How do services and supports for adolescents and adults with learning disabilities differ from those for children?

Read

These are important terms and concepts from Chapter Six. Match each term with the correct information.

a. intraindividual differences
b. hyperactivity or hyperkinesis
c. figure-ground discrimination
d. visual discrimination
e. auditory discrimination
f. auditory blending
g. auditory memory
h. auditory association
i. information processing
j. achievement discrepancy
k. norm-referenced assessment
l. criterion-referenced assessment
m. behavioral contract
n. token economy

6.1 ________ The act of distinguishing between different sounds.
6.2 ________ The act of blending parts of a word into a whole when speaking.
6.3 ________ The act of distinguishing one visual stimulus from another.
6.4 ________ The process of distinguishing an object from its background.
6.5 ________ An excess of behavior in inappropriate circumstances.
6.6 ________ Variation in a person's levels of performance across skill areas.
6.7 ________ A model used to study the way people acquire, remember, and manipulate information.
6.8 ________ The ability to connect verbally presented ideas or information.

6.9 __________ The ability to recall material presented verbally.
6.10 __________ Difference between performance and measured potential.
6.11 __________ Comparison of individual performance to the average of a large group.
6.12 __________ An agreement by which students receive tangible items that may be traded for rewards.
6.13 __________ Comparison of individual performance to a specific established level.
6.14 __________ An agreement that states if one behaves in a certain manner, a reward will be given.

Reflect

These terms are involved in defining and classifying learning disabilities.

a. learning disabilities
b. aphasia
c. dyslexia
d. perceptual-motor theories
e. language disability theories
f. Attention-Deficit/Hyperactivity Disorder (ADHD)
g. neurological disorder
h. perceptual disorders

6.15 _______ Attempts to explain a person's ability to interpret stimuli and then perform appropriate actions.
6.16 _______ A severe impairment in the ability to read.
6.17 _______ Acquired language disorder caused by brain damage, characterized by complete or partial impairment of language comprehension, formulation, and use.
6.18 _______ A generic educational term that includes a variety of different conditions resulting in behavioral and performance deficits.
6.19 _______ Theories related to a child's reception or production of language.
6.20 _______ A condition in which a child exhibits signs of developmentally inappropriate hyperactivity, impulsivity, and/or inattention.
6.21 _______ An inability to use one or more of the senses effectively in academic learning tasks.
6.22 _______ Problem pertaining to the nervous system.

Recite

Fill in the blanks with words that complete the meaning of the sentences.

6.23 Intervention strategies for people with learning disabilities have changed as professionals have come to view learning disabilities as a constellation of specific problems rather than as a __________ category.

6.24 The effectiveness of medication is questionable in treating ______________.

6.25 Programs focusing on disabilities such as perceptual, cognitive, attention, spoken language, reading, writing, and arithmetic are classified as ________ intervention.

6.26 Giving rewards for the performance of a specific behavior is a key element of the __________________contract.

6.27 Behavioral interventions, which are based on the fundamental principles of learning, have largely developed from the early work of experimental ________________.

6.28 When programs for adolescents with learning disabilities consider similar life goals to those relevant for nondisabled young people, ___________ intervention is being practiced.

6.29 The drugs most often used in medical intervention for controlling hyperactivity are in the ________ family.

6.30 Students with arithmetic learning difficulties may be effectively taught counting skills through the use of __________________ objects.

Review

This is good practice for an exam on material from Chapter Six.

6.31 Which statement best describes the area of learning disabilities?

a. It is the smallest category of exceptionality.
b. It is not defined as an exceptionality.
c. It is the largest category of exceptionality.
d. It includes children who are mentally retarded.

6.32 The classification of a child as learning disabled must be based on

a. the existence of a severe discrepancy between achievement and intellectual capacity
b. the existence of one or more neurological impairments
c. the existence of a physical handicap
d. the existence of environmental disadvantage

6.33 Evidence that hyperactive children have a higher level of activity than normal children is most easily seen in
  a. unstructured settings
  b. structured settings
  c. play settings
  d. all settings

6.34 Which term is used to denote difficulty in focusing on centrally important tasks or information?
  a. Selective attention problems
  b. Information processing problems
  c. Discrimination deficits
  d. Hyperkinesis

6.35 Which statement best describes the academic achievement of students with learning disabilities?
  a. They tend to be on the proper grade level.
  b. They generally achieve above their expected performance.
  c. They usually demonstrate poor reading skills while mastering other skills.
  d. They tend to be below their age-mates in achievement and perform below their potential.

6.36 Learning disabilities is a generic educational term related most accurately to
  a. many different disorders
  b. perceptual disorders
  c. minimal brain dysfunction
  d. visual discrimination disorders

6.37 The study of learning disabilities began as an attempt to help students having serious problems in
  a. reading
  b. mathematics
  c. science
  d. writing

6.38 In addition to receiving specific academic instruction, it is important for older students with learning problems to develop
  a. grade-level achievement in all academic areas
  b. higher cognition levels
  c. functional skills to compensate for certain skills not acquired earlier
  d. an understanding of the cause of their disability

6.39 Which is a compensatory strategy that could be used by a student with a learning disability?

a. Choosing vocational education in place of college
b. Eliminating problem academic areas from overall educational goals
c. Participating in computerized repetition and drill exercises until a skill is attained
d. Using a tape recorder in class to counter difficulties in listening and taking notes

6.40 Transition programs can effectively prepare students for college by teaching

a. advanced listening and note-taking skills
b. survival strategies and compensatory skills
c. ways to deal with college bureaucracy
d. ways to conceal learning problems

6.41 Which life goal should be considered by young adults in transition programs?

a. Further education in vocational or trade schools
b. Alternative goals, because learning disabled individuals will never be fully independent
c. Life goals similar to those of nondisabled people
d. Extended school years to attain high levels of academic achievement

6.42 Why do some students with learning disabilities experience social and behavioral difficulties?

a. Because they experience frustration and anxiety caused by repeated academic failure
b. Because behavior disorders tend to be the primary disability
c. Because they have limited adaptive behavior skills
d. Because their intellectual function is below average

6.43 An advantage of computer instruction for students with specific learning problems is

a. individual instruction and immediate feedback are provided
b. competition with other students is avoided
c. it keeps hyperactive students busy
d. individualized programs can replace special education

6.44 Compared with other disabilities, learning disabilities

a. can be easily identified
b. always involve a mild disorder
c. involve a homogeneous group of individuals
d. have generated more controversy than most other exceptionalities

6.45 The percentage of achievement-ability discrepancy needed for a student to be classified as learning disabled is

a. 10%
b. 20%
c. 25%
d. unspecified

6.46 Bill is a student with a learning disability. Sherry is a student with a behavior disorder. What attributes do they most likely share?

a. Poor home environment
b. Average to near average intelligence
c. Perceptual problems
d. Socioeconomic status

6.47 If Terry is exhibiting an intraindividual difference, he

a. has deficits in reading, math, and writing
b. performs at a level significantly lower than his age mates
c. performs at grade level in some areas, but below grade level in others
d. performs at a level that compares favorably with his age mates

6.48 A student with a visual-perception problem

a. typically cannot identify a visual stimulus
b. may see a visual stimulus as unrelated parts
c. usually has an accompanying visual impairment
d. is usually placed in a remedial reading program

6.49 Bess has difficulty distinguishing between the sounds of words. For example, she cannot hear the difference between the words *thing* and *think* or *pat* and *bat*. Bess has a problem with

a. auditory blending
b. auditory association
c. auditory retention
d. auditory discrimination

6.50 Ritalin is often prescribed to control

a. hypoactivity
b. hyperactivity
c. perseveration
d. lethargia

6.51 The learning strategies approach generally teaches a student

a. skills for being an effective learner
b. how to strategically adapt socially
c. how to focus on his or her strengths
d. effective adult social skills

6.52 The ultimate purpose of assessment in learning disabilities is

a. to determine the appropriate learning disability classification
b. to determine the appropriate funding level administratively
c. To eliminate other possible disability categories
d. to appropriately screen, identify, and place students who requite services.

6.53 Norm-reference assessments

a. compare a student's performances to a specific criterion
b. are designed to help in educational programming
c. provide information on specific learning deficits
d. compare an individual's performance to his or her age mates

6.54 Criterion-referenced assessments are helpful

a. in comparing the student's abilities with peers
b. for planning instructional programming
c. for diagnosing categories of exceptionality
d. In determining average class achievement

6.55 The purpose of screening students suspected of having a learning problem is to determine

a. the proper placement for a child
b. the nature of the learning problem
c. if more investigation is necessary
d. appropriate intervention strategies

ANSWER KEY FOR CHAPTER SIX

READ

6.1 e
6.2 f
6.3 d
6.4 c
6.5 b
6.6 a
6.7 i
6.8 h
6.9 g
6.10 j
6.11 k
6.12 n
6.13 l
6.14 m

REFLECT

6.15 d
6.16 c
6.17 b
6.18 a
6.19 e
6.20 f
6.21 h
6.22 g

RECITE

6.23 generic
6.24 hyperactivity
6.25 instructional
6.26 behavioral
6.27 psychologists
6.28 transition
6.29 amphetamine
6.30 manipulative

REVIEW

6.31 c
6.32 a
6.33 b
6.34 a
6.35 d
6.36 a
6.37 a
6.38 c
6.39 d
6.40 b
6.41 c
6.42 a
6.43 a
6.44 d
6.45 d
6.46 b
6.47 c
6.48 b
6.49 d
6.50 b
6.51 a
6.52 d
6.53 d
6.54 b
6.55 c

Chapter Seven

People with Attention-Deficit/Hyperactivity Disorder (ADHD)

Preview

Attention-deficit hyperactivity disorder (ADHD) was often considered to be a symptom accompanying other conditions. It is now recognized as a variety of physical processes interacting with social, psychological, or environmental factors.

This chapter examines ADHD and other disabilities, ADHD definitions, as well as prevalence of ADHD. The assessment and diagnosis of ADHD, along with the major characteristics of the condition, are also described.

The authors discuss causation, with both biological and environmental influences having been identified in the etiology. The chapter ends with an overview of interventions effective during the elementary school years and then those interventions useful during adolescence and adulthood.

Question

Seek to answer these questions in your reading.

What three behavioral symptoms are commonly associated with ADHD?

What are two ways in which the behavior of children with ADHD detrimentally affects instructional settings?

What four other areas of disability are often found to be combined with ADHD?

Why are the three major types of ADHD according to the DSM-IV?

What are two prevalence estimates for ADHD that characterize the difference in occurrence by gender?

What are the two broad categories of assessment information useful in diagnosing ADHD?

What three areas of difficulty present challenges for individuals with ADHD?

What are three possible causes of ADHD?

What two approaches to intervention appear to show positive results with individuals having ADHD?

Read

Match these terms with their correct definitions.

a. comorbidity
b. Other Health Impairments
c. executive function
d. frontal lobes
e. Child Behavior Checklist (CBCL)
f. Tourette's Syndrome

7.1 __________ The ability to monitor and regulate one's own behavior.
7.2 __________ A condition characterized by motor or verbal ties.
7.3 __________ An instrument often used to assess ADHD.
7.4 __________ The parts of the brain nearest the forehead.
7.5 __________ IDEA category under which students with ADHD are eligible for services.
7.6 __________ Two conditions occurring together.

Reflect

Here are more useful names and terms you should know.

a. basal ganglia
b. cognitive-behavioral therapy
c. multimodal treatments
d. cerebellum
e. methylphenidate
f. hyperactivity

7.7 __________ The part of the brain that coordinates muscular movement.
7.8 __________ The primary characteristics of ADHD.
7.9 __________ Sections of the brain near the stem, where the spinal cord meets brain matter.

7.10 __________ The generic name for Ritalin, a stimulant mediation.
7.11 __________ Therapies based on behavioral techniques combined with efforts to change thought patterns.
7.12 __________ Multiple treatment approaches.

Recite

Complete the sentences with words from the chapter.

7.13 People with ADHD face significant challenges at every_______________.

7.14 It is estimated that ADHD is a lifetime disability for about_______ of those who are affected.

7.15 The American Psychiatric Association includes _______________ subcategories.

7.16 The male-to-female ADHD ratios range from 2:1 to__________.

7.17 More than _______________ of those with ADHD demonstrate comorbidity with some other identifiable condition.

7.18 While children with ADHD often struggle academically, they tend not to exhibit specific difficulties in ______.

Review

For each item choose the best of the four answers.

7.19 Being overly active seems to affect about ________ of the children diagnosed with ADHD.

a. 70%
b. 50%
c. 80%
d. 30%

7.20 The skill areas that students with ADHD have the most difficulty are

a. self-management and thinking ahead
b. controlling anger and thinking ahead
c. thinking ahead and social skills
d. focusing attention and thinking ahead

7.21 The Diagnostic Interview Schedule for Children is appropriately used as part of a(n)

a. initial reference
b. final diagnostic evaluation
c. comprehensive clinical interview
d. follow-up screening

7.22 Thinking through one's actions to see what the effects of certain behaviors might be can be likened to

a. behavioral inhibition
b. executive function
c. impulse control
d. all of the above

7.23 Evidence is emerging that pharmacological control of behavioral challenges associated with ADHD are

a. more effective than nonmedical interventions
b. less effective than nonmedial interventions
c. as effective as nonmedical interventions
d. only effective in conjunction with nonmedical interventions

7.24 Psychostimulants appear to result in behavioral improvement for about ______ of children with ADHD.

a. 50%
b. 30%
c. 80%
d. 60%

7.25 Estimates suggest that ________ of those diagnosed as ADHD during childhood continue to be challenged as adults.

a. 50% to 90%
b. 20% to 70%
c. 40% to 80%
d. 30% to 80%

7.26 Medications do not improve the behavior of about ________ of children with ADHD.

a. 50%
b. 20%
c. 40%
d. 70%

7.27 The social relationships of youngsters with ADHD and their peers is

a. often difficult
b. usually satisfactory
c. often very good
d. characterized by aggression

ANSWER KEY FOR CHAPTER SEVEN

READ

7.1 c
7.2 f
7.3 e
7.4 d
7.5 b
7.6 a

REFLECT

7.7 d
7.8 f
7.9 a
7.10 e
7.11 b
7.12 c

RECITE

7.13 age
7.14 half
7.15 3
7.16 10:1
7.17 70%
7.18 memory

REVIEW

7.19 b
7.20 a
7.21 c
7.22 d
7.23 a
7.24 c
7.25 d
7.26 b
7.27 a

Chapter Eight

People with Emotional or Behavior Disorders

Preview

This chapter introduces five factors that influence the ways in which behavior may be evaluated. The authors explain why emotional or behavior disorders are difficult to study, discussing variables that affect many different types of behavior that may be exhibited or suppressed when an individual has a behavior disorder. Typically, definitions of EBD refer to behavior in terms of frequency and contexts.

Child, adolescent and adult behavior disorders are frequently grouped into two broad, overlapping categories: externalizing and internalizing disorders. However, there is no consistent, standardized set of criteria for delineating the nature and severity of emotional or behavior disorders. Three methods of approaching classification are outlined: statistically derived, clinically derived, and severity based.

The authors describe the characteristics of people with emotional or behavior disorders--including intelligence, adaptive and social behavior, and academic achievement. The causes of disorders are reviewed from five perspectives: biological, psychoanalytical, behavioral, phenomenological, and sociological-ecological. The chapter includes an overview of assessment and intervention programs that are implemented during early childhood, elementary school years, and the adolescent years. Issues involved with placing students with behavior disorders in inclusion programs are briefly discussed. The chapter closes by summarizing promising practices for addressing chronic behavior problems.

Question

After thoroughly previewing Chapter Eight, you will be able to answer the following questions:

What five factors influence the ways behavior can be viewed?

What differentiates externalizing disorders from internalizing disorders?

What six parts are essential to defining serious emotional disturbances or behavior disorders?

Why are classification systems important to professionals who diagnose, treat, and educate individuals with behavior disorders?

What five general characteristics are typical of children and youth with behavior disorders?

What is known about the causes of behavior disorders?

What three outcomes are achieved through a functional behavioral assessment?

What five guiding principles are associated with systems of care?

What five factors ought to be considered when placing a student with behavior disorders in general education and related settings?

What are 12 promising practices for dealing with challenging behavior?

Read

Following are some important vocabulary words from Chapter Seven. Match the terms with their meanings.

a. externalizing disorders
b. internalizing disorders
c. conduct disorder
d. anxiety disorder
e. immaturity
f. socialized aggression
g. undersocialized aggressive
h. strength-based assessment
i. positive behavioral assessment
j. screening
k. task analysis
l. wraparound services

8.1 ______ Involves preoccupation, short attention span, passivity, and daydreaming.
8.2 ______ Involves social withdrawal, seclusiveness, shyness, and sensitivity.
8.3 ______ Involves overt aggression, disruptiveness, negativism, irresponsibility, and defiance of authority.
8.4 ______ Involves gang activity, cooperative stealing, and truancy.
8.5 ______ Involves those who are impulsive, hyperactive, irritable, and tenaciously stubborn.
8.6 ______ Directs behaviors more at oneself than at others.
8.7 ______ Directs behaviors more at others than at oneself.
8.8 ______ Rather than deficit-oriented, this approach focuses on strengths.
8.9 ______ Approach that addresses the features and factors related to challenging behaviors.
8.10 ______ Breaks down behaviors into their most elementary parts for teaching.
8.11 ______ Providing the support needed for students and their families to solve their problems.

8.12 ______ Identifies infants, children, and youths who are most in need of treatment.

Reflect

Try to match each term with the correct definition. If you get all eight, you're doing great.

a. Pervasive Developmental Disorders
b. Functional behavioral assessment
c. DSM-IV-R
d. curriculum of noninstruction
e. curriculum of control
f. tic disorders
g. elective mutism

8.13 ______ Program focused on controlling behaviors of students.
8.14 ______ Severe delays in the acquisition of motor, language, cognitive, and social skills.
8.15 ______ Persistent refusal to talk.
8.16 ______ Category of disorders involving stereotyped movements or vocalizations.
8.17 ______ Identifying the functions of a student's behavior in relationship to various settings.
8.18 ______ Program that is restrictive and punitive rather than focusing on developing new behaviors.
8.19 ______ Manual used by medical and psychological personnel to classify people with emotional or behavior disorders.

Recite

Fill in the blanks with appropriate words from Chapter Seven. This section is a real test of your knowledge.

8.20 In most school environments, children are considered for screening only after a concerned or perplexed teacher has initiated a ____________ for them.

8.21 A behavioral-analysis technique in which a well-trained observer compares behaviors exhibited by different students is ______________.

8.22 Identifying the function that a behavior serves in meeting the needs of an individual is the purpose of _________________.

8.23 Students with behavior disorders are ________ times more likely than other students to be arrested in school.

8.24 Students with behavior disorders are more likely to be ________, male, and African-American.

8.25 A new instrument, the ___________, provides teachers with a means for choosing developmentally appropriate long-term goals to gain behavioral competence.

8.26 The majority of students with behavior disorders receive instruction _________ of general education classrooms.

8.27 "We will help you reach your potential in spite of the terrible things you have done," is the first principle of ____________.

8.28 The current systems of care are characterized by ________________ collaboration.

Review

Choose the best of four answers. If you get these correct you should do well on the test.

8.29 A major influence on what is viewed as appropriate or inappropriate behavior is
a. the effect of behavior on others
b. the context in which behavior occurs
c. the type of behavior
d. the frequency of behavior

8.30 Which of the following behaviors is an externalizing disorder?
a. Feeling abandoned
b. Hearing voices
c. Spitting on a sibling
d. Experiencing test anxiety

8.31 Types of behavior disorders that involve behavior directed at others are classified as
a. internalizing disorders
b. pervasive developmental disorders
c. separation anxiety disorders
d. externalizing disorders

8.32 According to IDEA, a child is considered behaviorally disordered when behavior which occurs over a long period of time and to a marked degree adversely affects the individual's

a. social adjustment
b. intellectual capacity
c. educational performance
d. health

8.33 Children who are unable to attend to tasks or control their level of physical activity have

a. Attention-Deficit Hyperactive Disorder
b. conduct disorders
c. tic disorders
d. anxiety disorders

8.34 Which statement is true of special education programs?

a. The number of children with behavior disorders participating in programs has declined over the years.
b. Programs for children with behavior disorders have grown rapidly in rural areas.
c. One-fifth of all students in special day schools and one-half of all students in residential facilities are children with behavior disorders.
d. Female students with behavior disorders outnumber males by at least two to one.

8.35 The best predictor of a behaviorally disordered child's academic and social achievement is

a. maturity level
b. language competency
c. intellectual capacity
d. level of adaptive behavior

8.36 Observations of children with behavior disorders indicate that academic performance is

a. not consistent with their intellectual ability as represented by IQ scores
b. subaverage as predicted by their intellectual deficits
c. above average in relation to their nonhandicapped peers
d. impossible to measure due to hyperactive behaviors and distractibility

8.37 Which assessment technique employs a trained observer to count and record instances of a specific problem behavior?

a. Rating scales
b. Direct observation
c. Formal interview
d. Personality inventory

8.38 Which of the following factors critically affect the emergence of behavior disorders?

a. Malnutrition
b. Incompetent parenting
c. Child abuse and neglect
d. All of the above

8.39 Which two important features must be present in a special education classroom for children with moderate to severe behavior disorders?

a. High degree of structure and frequent feedback to students.
b. High degree of structure and isolated instruction.
c. Frequent monitoring of student performance and low degree of peer interaction.
d. Consistent therapeutic intervention and infrequent use of reward systems.

8.40 Research on youth with behavior disorders indicates that

a. the drop-out rate is about 50 percent
b. 41% are employed two years after leaving high school
c. about 17% go on to college
d. all of the above are true

8.41 Statistically derived classification systems typically describe individuals who

a. evidence pervasive developmental disorders
b. evidence feeding and eating disorders
c. evidence anxiety-withdrawal and conduct disorders
d. evidence clinically substantiated behavior disorders

8.42 What major purpose is served through classification systems?

a. They provide an accurate means for assessing intervention effectiveness.
b. They provide a means for describing various behavior disorders.
c. They provide valuable information about the effective treatments.
d. They provide means for predicting treatment outcomes.

8.43 Disorders identified in the DSM-IV overlap with the following conditions

a. mental retardation, autism, and attention deficit disorders
b. mental retardation, autism, and immaturity disorders
c. mental retardation, attention deficit disorders, and anxiety-withdrawal disorders
d. mental retardation, attention deficit disorders, and socialized aggression

8.44 Which theoretical approach explains behavior as a function of instincts or early traumatic experiences?

a. Biological approach
b. Psychoanalystical approach
c. Behavioral approach
d. Phenomenological approach

8.45 The framework which explains behavior disorders in terms of an individual's self-perception is known as

a. behavioral approach
b. biological approach
c. phenomenological approach
d. sociological-ecological approach

8.46 What usually takes place prior to a formal referral?

a. The behavior disorder is diagnosed.
b. Observations are completed using behavioral checklists.
c. A number of parent-teacher conferences take place.
d. Behavior modification techniques are implemented.

8.47 Inclusion of students with behavior disorders is greatly enhanced when general education personnel receive

a. additional pay
b. timely, intensive, consultation
c. a reduced teaching assignment
d. increased parental support

8.48 The aggression replacement training (ART) program emphasizes

a. social skills training
b. moral education
c. self-management
d. All of the above

ANSWER KEY FOR CHAPTER EIGHT

READ

8.1 e
8.2 d
8.3 c
8.4 f
8.5 g
8.6 b
8.7 a
8.8 h
8.9 i
8.10 k
8.11 l
8.12 j

REFLECT

8.13 e
8.14 a
8.15 g
8.16 f
8.17 b
8.18 d
8.19 c

RECITE

8.20 referral
8.21 direct observation
8.22 functional behavioral assessment
8.23 13
8.24 economically disadvantaged
8.25 Behavioral Objective Sequence
8.26 outside
8.27 individualized care
8.28 family-provider

REVIEW

8.29 b
8.30 c
8.31 d
8.32 c
8.33 a
8.34 c
8.35 c
8.36 a
8.37 b
8.38 d
8.39 a
8.40 d
8.41 c
8.42 b
8.43 a
8.44 b
8.45 c
8.46 c
8.47 b
8.48 d

Chapter Nine

People with Mental Retardation

Preview

According to the American Association on Mental Retardation (AAMR), mental retardation is defined in relation to three components: intelligence, adaptive skills, and age of onset. In order to more clearly represent the diversity of functioning levels and characteristics of persons with mental retardation, four classification systems are explained in the chapter: severity of condition, educability expectations, medical descriptors, and level of needed support.

Chapter Nine details the characteristics of mental retardation in seven areas: learning and memory, self-regulation, adaptive skills, academic achievement, motivation, speech-language development, and physical characteristics.

Possible causes of mental retardation that are discussed include sociocultural influences, biomedical factors, metabolic and nutritional factors, behavioral factors, and unknown prenatal influences. Recent preventive measures have focused on immunizing against disease, monitoring maternal nutritional habits during pregnancy, providing appropriate prenatal care, and screening for genetic disorders at birth.

The importance of early childhood education is stressed. Educational programming for elementary school age children is concerned with decreasing dependence on others (motor development, self-care, and functional academics) and teaching adaptation to the environment (social skills, communication). The goals of educational programming for adolescents include increasing personal independence and enhancing opportunities for participation in the local community, as well as preparing for employment and successful transition into adulthood.

Educational placement, whether in a segregated or inclusive setting, has been a critical concern for many years. Medical and social services are both needed to enable people who are mentally retarded to function successfully as part of the community.

Question

After a thorough preview of Chapter Nine, you should know the answers to these questions:

What are the three components of the current AAMR definition of mental retardation?

What are the four approaches to classifying people who are mentally retarded?

What is the prevalence of mental retardation?

What are the four intellectual and adaptive skills characteristics of individuals with mental retardation?

What are the academic, motivational, speech/language, and physical characteristics of students with mental retardation?

What are the most prevalent causes of mental retardation?

What four measures are being implemented to prevent mental retardation?

Why is there such a crucial need for early intervention services for children with mental retardation?

What are the five skill areas for elementary-age children with mental retardation?

What are the four educational goals for adolescents with mental retardation?

Why is the inclusion of students who are mentally retarded with their non-disabled peers an important part of an appropriate educational experience?

In what ways are medical and social services meeting the diverse needs of people with mental retardation?

Read

Try to match these important terms and concepts from Chapter Nine with the corresponding definitions. These terms are important to know.

a. mental retardation
b. American Association on Mental Retardation (AAMR)
c. adaptive skill
d. age of onset
e. functional reading
f. educable
g. trainable
h. custodial
i. learning set
j. rehearsal strategies
k. nature vs. nurture
l. "cultural-familial"

9.1 _______ Term that refers to learning how to learn and developing the ability to apply what is learned to a new experience.

9.2 ________ Level of mental retardation, based on educability expectation, which involves measured intelligence of 40 to 55.

9.3 ________ Level of mental retardation, based on educability expectation, which includes measured intelligence below 40.

9.4 ________ Organization that developed a widely accepted definition of mental retardation.

9.5 ________ A condition which results in subaverage intellectual functioning.

9.6 ________ Term that refers to a person's ability to be socially appropriate and personally responsible.

9.7 ________ Having enough sight vocabulary to scan printed materials and glean key information.

9.8 ________ Level of mental retardation, based on educability expectation, which includes measured intelligence of 55 to about 70.

9.9 ________ Time during which mental retardation may begin.

9.10 ________ Controversy over whether sociocultural factors or genetic factors are most influential in causing mental retardation.

9.11 ________ Plans or tactics for practicing material to be learned.

9.12 ________ Position that mental retardation may be attributed to both sociocultural and genetic factors.

These terms all relate to infection, intoxication, or chromosomal abnormalities. Try these without your book.

m. maternal infections
n. congenital rubella
o. congenital syphilis
p. toxoplasmosis
q. intoxication
r. Fetal Alcohol Syndrome
s. anticonvulsant
t. Rhogam
u. encephalitis
v. Down syndrome
w. Trisomy 21

9.13 ________ A type of Down syndrome in which the chromosomal pairs do not separate properly.

9.14 ________ German measles contracted by a mother during pregnancy.

9.15 ________ Infection in a mother during pregnancy.

9.16 ________ Excessive level of toxic agent.

9.17 ________ Syphilis transmitted from pregnant mother to her unborn child.

9.18 ________ Infection caused by protozoa carried in raw meat and fecal material.

9.19 ________ Medication associated with infant malformations.

9.20 ________ Damage caused to fetus by maternal consumption of alcohol.

9.21 ________ Treatment used to combat incompatibility in blood types.
9.22 ________ Condition that results from chromosomal abnormalities.
9.23 ________ An inflammation of brain tissue.

These terms all relate to gestation disorders, traumas, or physical agents.

aa. prematurity
bb. low birth weight
cc. anencephaly
dd. hydrocephalus
ee. breech presentation
ff. anoxia
gg. precipitous birth
hh. metabolic disorders
ii. phenylketonuria (PKU)
jj. galactosemia
kk. neurofibromatosis
ll. tuberous sclerosis

9.24 ________ Lack of oxygen during delivery.
9.25 ________ Position of fetus with buttocks toward the cervix.
9.26 ________ Excess of cerebrospinal fluid accumulating in the skull.
9.27 ________ Delivery involving brief labor.
9.28 ________ Metabolic disorder which causes mental retardation if untreated.
9.29 ________ Defects in the body's ability to process substances normally.
9.30 ________ Delivery before 35 weeks.
9.31 ________ An infant weighing less than 5 1/2 pounds at birth.
9.32 ________ A partial or complete absence of cerebral tissue.
9.33 ________ A birth defect that does not appear until later in life and is characterized by tumors on many organs.
9.34 ________ An inherited disorder resulting in tumors.
9.35 ________ A disorder which causes an infant to have difficulty processing lactose.

Reflect

These terms and concepts apply to intervention for people who are mentally retarded. You should know all of these!

a. infant stimulation programs
b. supported employment
c. Project Head Start
d. Apgar scoring

e. augmentative communication
f. related services
g. normalization

9.36 ________ Use of sign language and/or language boards.
9.37 ________ Principle emphasizing that people with disabilities should be part of mainstream society.
9.38 ________ Services not usually classified as educational.
9.39 ________ Screening procedure used with infants.
9.40 ________ A prevention program that attempts to identify and teach high-risk children before they enter public school.
9.41 ________ Methodology that provides an array of visual, auditory, and physical stimuli.
9.42 ________ An opportunity for individuals with mental retardation to work in the community made possible by use of additional help/support.

Recite

Use words relating to the prevention of mental retardation to fill in the blanks. Good luck with these.

9.43 A condition caused by nutritional inadequacy in a pregnant mother which may cause fetal problems is maternal ________________.

9.44 A procedure that evaluates an infant on heart rate, respiratory condition, muscle tone, reflex irritability, and color is ________ scoring.

9.45 A search among members of a population for people possessing certain genotypes is genetic ____________.

9.46 Protecting family members from contracting serious illness and guarding against the mother becoming ill during pregnancy can be achieved through ________________.

9.47 A process often carried out when there is some reason to believe that a person carries a genetic abnormality is genetic ______________.

9.48 A rare genetic condition typically associated with mental retardation, but also characterized by unique language abilities is ________.

9.49 The time immediately following birth is the ______________ period.

9.50 Amniocentesis, fetoscopy, and ultrasound are methods used after conception to determine the presence of genetic ________________.

Review

Try these questions to test your knowledge of Chapter Nine. Mastery of these items suggests you know your stuff!

9.51 Which are the three major components of the AAMR definition of mental retardation?

a. Adaptive skills, age of onset, and physical ability
b. Medical condition, hereditary factors, and intelligence
c. Intelligence, adaptive skills, and prenatal history
d. Intelligence, adaptive skills, and age of onset

9.52 The 1992 AAMR definition of mental retardation places emphasis on

a. the role of chromosomal abnormalities as a casual factor
b. incurability of the condition
c. intellectual dysfunction as a primary indicator of mental retardation
d. intensity of needed supports for family, school and community living

9.53 Which of the classification systems discussed in the text have traditionally used the term *trainable mentally retarded*?

a. Severity of the condition
b. Educability expectation
c. Medical descriptors
d. Adaptive skill expectations

9.54 What is the primary characteristic of mental retardation?

a. Intellectual deficiency
b. Maladaptive functioning
c. Physical impairment
d. Bizarre speech

9.55 In motivating students with mental retardation, Dever and Knapczyk (1997) suggested

a. changing the objective
b. rewarding the learner for doing what they're supposed to do
c. developing a different activity that is more inherently motivating
d. All of the above

9.56 One major goal of an education program for adolescents with mental retardation is

a. increasing academic performance
b. enhancing communication skills
c. participating in family counseling
d. increasing personal independence

9.57 The principle of normalization states that individuals with mental retardation

a. must be offered the same educational opportunities as nondisabled students through the process of mainstreaming
b. must have opportunities available to them in everyday life that are as close as possible to those available to nondisabled people
c. must participate in segregated special school programs to benefit from highly individualized educational opportunities
d. must seek employment immediately upon leaving high school

9.58 Which is an example of teaching functional academic skills to students with mental retardation?

a. Teaching words that are often encountered in the environment
b. Teaching math skills through drilling exercises
c. Teaching a basic academic curriculum
d. Teaching words that are found only in school textbooks

9.59 Social skills training emphasizes the importance of

a. using appropriate communication
b. learning problem-solving
c. decision making skills
d. all of the above

9.60 Which of the following statements regarding Phenylketonuria (PKU) is true?

a. PKU causes minimal damage to the central nervous system
b. Mental retardation can be prevented if PKU is treated promptly
c. Mental retardation caused by PKU may be reversed through surgery
d. PKU cannot be treated until the infant is at least 12 months old

9.61 Which condition is caused by excessive use of alcohol by a pregnant mother?

a. Down syndrome
b. Hydrocephalus
c. Fetal Alcohol Syndrome
d. Neurofibromatosis

9.62 Mario needs continual daily support in at least some environments, including work and home. To be effective, these supports must not be time-limited. AAMR would classify Mario's required supports as

a. intermittent
b. limited
c. extensive
d. pervasive

9.63 A term that best denotes effectiveness with which a person with mental retardation is able to manage his or her own behavior is

a. learned helplessness
b. self-advocacy
c. self-concept
d. self-regulation

9.64 In general, the weakest academic area for students who are mentally retarded is

a. math computation
b. reading comprehension
c. spelling
d. handwriting

9.65 "No matter how hard I try I will not succeed" is a statement closely associated with which of the following terms?

a. Outer-directed behavior
b. Underdeveloped self-concept
c. Learned helplessness
d. Self-determination

9.66 Non-institutionalized people in the United States constitute

a. the fastest growing segment of the population
b. about 6.6 million people or about 3% of the population
c. about 1.9 million people or about .78% of the population
d. about 7.5 million people, or about 5% of the population

ANSWER KEY FOR CHAPTER NINE

READ

9.1 i
9.2 g
9.3 h
9.4 b
9.5 a
9.6 c
9.7 e
9.8 f
9.9 d
9.10 k
9.11 j
9.12 l
9.13 w
9.14 n
9.15 m
9.16 q
9.17 o
9.18 p
9.19 s
9.20 r
9.21 t
9.22 v
9.23 u
9.24 ff
9.25 ee
9.26 dd
9.27 gg
9.28 ii
9.29 hh
9.30 aa
9.31 bb
9.32 cc
9.33 kk
9.34 ll
9.35 jj

REFLECT

9.36 e
9.37 g
9.38 f
9.39 d
9.40 c
9.41 a
9.42 b

RECITE

9.43 malnutrition
9.44 Apgar
9.45 screening
9.46 immunization
9.47 counseling
9.48 William's syndrome
9.49 neonatal
9.50 abnormalities

REVIEW

9.51 d
9.52 d
9.53 b
9.54 a
9.55 d
9.56 d
9.57 b
9.58 a
9.59 d
9.60 b
9.61 c
9.62 c
9.63 d
9.64 b
9.65 c
9.66 c

Chapter Ten

People with Communication Disorders

Preview

This chapter addresses two major interrelated components of communication: speech and language. Speech is the audible production of language, and language is the intended message contained in speech. Problems in either can significantly affect a person's daily life.

Language disorders occur when individuals experience a serious disruption in the language process: a breakdown in the ability to understand or express ideas in the communication system that is being used. The authors address both *receptive* and *expressive* problems as well as aphasia, which may include elements of both. Receptive and expressive problems are often intertwined; thus causation is difficult to determine. Treatment of language disorders must consider both the nature of the problem and the manner in which an individual is affected.

The authors define a speech disorder as a behavior that is sufficiently deviant from normal speaking patterns that communication is impaired. Speech disorders are discussed under the categories of fluency disorders, delayed speech, articulation disorders, and voice disorders. The chapter explains some of the features of each category, including characteristics, causes, intervention strategies, and prevalence estimates.

Question

After previewing the material on language and speech disorders, you should be able to answer the following questions:

In what four ways are speech, language, and communication interrelated?

In what two ways are language delay and language disorder different?

What are the three factors thought to be involved in causing language disorders?

In what two ways do treatment approaches for language disorders generally differ for children and adults?

What three factors are thought to be involved in causing stuttering?

In what two ways do learning theory and home environment relate to delayed speech?

What two reasons make some professionals reluctant to treat functional articulation disorders in young school children?

Read

These are important terms and concepts from Chapter Ten. Match them with their meanings.

a. communication
b. speech
c. language
d. phonology
e. syntax
f. morphology
g. semantics
h. pragmatics
i. speech disorders
j. fluency disorders
k. cluttering
l. stuttering

10.1 ________ The ways in which words are combined and sequenced to produce meaning in phrases, clauses, and sentences.
10.2 ________ The system of speech sounds.
10.3 ________ The intended message contained in speaking.
10.4 ________ Processes involved in sending and receiving messages, encoding and decoding the meaning of those messages.
10.5 ________ The audible production of language.
10.6 ________ Study of the use of language in social contexts.
10.7 ________ Behavior that is sufficiently deviant from the norm to interfere with communication.
10.8 ________ Study concerned with communicative and social functions of language.
10.9 ________ The form and internal structure of words.
10.10 ________ Disorder characterized by excessively rapid, disorganized speaking.
10.11 ________ Speech which involves abnormal repetitions, prolongations, and hesitations.
10.12 ________ Type of disorder where the rhythm of speaking is excessively interrupted.

Here are more terms for you to match and study.

a. delayed speech
b. articulation disorders
c. infantile perseveration
d. negativism

e. functional articulation disorders
f. cleft palate
g. malocclusion
h. prosthetic
i. voice disorder
j. hyponasality or denasality
k. hypernasality

10.13 ________ A deficit in speaking proficiency which causes the individual to perform like someone much younger.
10.14 ________ The articulation aspect of delayed speech.
10.15 ________ Abnormality in the sound production aspect of speech, resulting in inaccurate or otherwise inappropriate pronunciation.
10.16 ________ Withdrawal and refusal to speak which results when demands on a young child exceed his or her performance level.
10.17 ________ Problems not due to structural defects or neurological problems, but more likely the result of environmental or psychological influences.
10.18 ________ A device that replaces a missing or malfunctioning part of the body.
10.19 ________ A normal fit of the upper and lower dental structures.
10.20 ________ A gap in the soft palate and the roof of the mouth.
10.21 ________ Defect in resonance where too little air passes through the nasal cavity.
10.22 ________ Defect in resonance where too much air passes through the nasal cavity.
10.23 ________ A condition in which a person speaks with a voice that differs in pitch, loudness, or quality from the voices of others of the same sex and age in a cultural group.

Reflect

Here are some more terms for you to review.

a. language disorder
b. language delay
c. aphasia
d. receptive language disorder
e. expressive language disorder
f. developmental aphasia
g. assistive, alternative, or augmentative communication
h. individualized language plan (ILP)

10.24 ______ A language disorder in children, caused by brain damage, characterized by complete or partial impairment of language comprehension, use, etc.
10.25 ______ Difficulties in language production.
10.26 ______ Difficulties in comprehending what others say.
10.27 ______ An acquired language disorder caused by brain damage.
10.28 ______ A term used when the sequence of language development is seriously

interrupted.

10.29 ______ A term used when the normal rate of language development is interrupted, but the developmental sequence remains intact.

10.30 ______ A non-speech means of communication.

10.31 ______ A language-training program tailored to an individual's needs.

Recite

Supply the word(s) which best complete the meanings of the sentences.

10.32 Speech and language are two of a number of components of ______________.

10.33 There are components of communication that involve language but not ______________.

10.34 There may be speech that does not involve ____________________.

10.35 From a general perspective, emotional problems, neurological problems, and learned behavior can contribute to ____________________.

10.36 People who stutter learn their speech patterns as an outgrowth of normal nonfluency when speech ______________ is occurring.

10.37 In language delay, the sequence of development is intact but the rate of development is ________.

10.38 One factor thought to contribute to language disorders is physical trauma or accident creating _______ damage.

10.39 Treatment for children with language disorders generally addresses initial acquisition or learning of ______________.

Review

This exercise will help you learn the concepts presented in Chapter Ten. Selecting the best answer will help you prepare for a test on the material.

10.40 An example of a language disorder is
- a. stuttering
- b. aphasia
- c. cluttering
- d. infantile preservation

10.41 Which component of communication involves memory, learning, message reception and processing, and expressive skills?

a. Articulation
b. Receptive language
c. Speech
d. Language

10.42 The largest category of all speech disorders is

a. articulation disorders
b. stuttering
c. malocclusion
d. aphasia

10.43 Functional articulation disorders are generally thought to be caused by

a. faulty learning
b. physical deformity
c. brain dysfunction
d. hereditary factors

10.44 Approaches to voice disorder treatment depend on

a. the person's wishes
b. the teacher's plans
c. the parent's feelings
d. causation

10.45 Children with receptive language problems are often recognized as having a problem when they fail to

a. learn to read
b. follow directions given by adults
c. learn to speak
d. respond to loud noises

10.46 The interchange of ideas, opinions or facts between senders and receivers is referred to as

a. communication
b. talking
c. speech
d. language

10.47 Which of the following is an example of speech without language?

a. Using sign language
b. Using a communication board
c. Training a bird to talk
d. Writing a note

10.48 Many articulation problems evident in young children are developmental, and speech may improve with

a. drug therapy
b. age
c. surgery
d. punishment

10.49 In a language disorder, the sequence of development is

a. interrupted
b. intact
c. irrelevant
d. delayed

10.50 ______________ is concerned with the form and internal structure of words (e.g. past tense singular form).

a. Morphology
b. Syntax
c. Semantics
d. Pragmatics

10.51 Which term denotes the rules governing sentence structure?

a. Syntax
b. Morphology
c. Semantics
d. Phonology

10.52 Which category of speech disorders is characterized by repeated interruptions, hesitations, or repetitions that interrupt the flow of communication?

a. Articulation disorders
b. Delayed speech
c. Voice disorders
d. Fluency disorder

10.53 Which statement best describes the interaction between communication, language, and speech?

a. Each component exists in isolation.
b. The development of these components overlaps.
c. Communication includes the components of speech and language.
d. Speech does not involve language.

10.54 Between three and six months of age, babies begin to do which of the following?

a. Echo all sounds
b. Say their first words
c. Show pleasure through cooing
d. Babble

10.55 Treatment approaches for people who stutter have increasingly focused on
a. counseling
b. biofeedback
c. relaxation
d. direct behavioral therapy

10.56 Functional articulation disorders are distinguished from structural disorders by
a. the presence of brain damage with functional disorders
b. the fact that functional disorders are easier to treat
c. the lack of physical deformities with functional disorders
d. the severity of the disorders

10.57 An oral malformation which causes a reduced division of the nasal and mouth cavities is known as a/an
a. cleft palate
b. absent larynx
c. overbite
d. jaw misalignment

10.58 When the pitch, loudness and quality of a person's speech interferes with the listener's attention to the message, the person may be experiencing a/an
a. articulation disorder
b. voice disorder
c. fluency disorder
d. speech disorder

10.59 About what percentage of those receiving services through I.D.E.A. were classified as speech or language impaired in 1995-1996?
a. 13%
b. 17%
c. 19%
d. 28%

10.60 Receptive language disorders are characterized by difficulties in
a. hearing what others say
b. using spoken language
c. formulating language
d. comprehending what others say

10.61 Students who repeatedly use the same words in a variety of situations may be experiencing what type of disorder?
a. Receptive language disorder
b. Expressive language disorder
c. Articulation disorder
d. Voice disorder

10.62 Delayed speech is most often associated with which of the following?

a. Hearing impairment
b. Regressed growth of the Vermis
c. Gonadal dysplacia
d. Developmental inconsistency: physical type

ANSWER KEY FOR CHAPTER TEN

READ

10.1 e
10.2 d
10.3 c
10.4 a
10.5 b
10.6 h
10.7 i
10.8 g
10.9 f
10.10 k

10.11 l
10.12 j
10.13 m
10.14 o
10.15 n
10.16 p
10.17 q
10.18 t
10.19 s
10.20 r
10.21 v
10.22 w
10.23 u

RECITE

10.32 communication
10.33 speech
10.34 language
10.35 stuttering
10.36 development
10.37 interrupted
10.38 neurological
10.39 language

REFLECT

10.24 f
10.25 e
10.26 d
10.27 c
10.28 a
10.29 b
10.30 g
10.31 h

REVIEW

10.40 b
10.41 d
10.42 a
10.43 a
10.44 d
10.45 b
10.46 a
10.47 c
10.48 b
10.49 a
10.50 a
10.51 a
10.52 d
10.53 c
10.54 d
10.55 d
10.56 c
10.57 a
10.58 b
10.59 c
10.60 d
10.61 b
10.62 a

Chapter Eleven

People with Severe and Multiple Disabilities

Preview

This chapter presents several definitions of severe and multiple disabilities as well as describing the terms *dual diagnosis* and *dual sensory impairment.* Information regarding the prevalence and causation of severe and multiple disabilities is also presented.

The characteristics of people with severe and multiple disabilities, including their intelligence and academic achievement, adaptive skills, speech and language skills, physical and health attributes, and vision and hearing abilities are described. Assessment, both traditional and functional, as it relates to people with sever and multiple disabilities, is explained.

Services and supports for people with severe and multiple disabilities at various life stages are presented. Emphasis is given to the features that characterize quality programs. The four attributes of successful inclusion efforts are further described.

The chapter concludes with a discussion of the four bioethical dilemmas that people with severe and multiple disabilities and their families may face.

Question

After a careful preview, you should be able to answer these questions:

What are the three components of the TASH definition of severe disabilities?

What are the definitions of multiple disabilities and deafness-blindness in IDEA?

What prevalence has been estimated, and what cause(s) have been suggested for severe and multiple disabilities?

What are the characteristics of persons with severe and multiple disabilities?

What is the functional approach to assessing the needs of people with severe and multiple disabilities?

What are the features of effective services and supports for children with severe and multiple disabilities during early childhood?

What are the features of effective services and supports for children with severe and multiple disabilities during the elementary school years?

What are four important outcomes in planning for the transition from school to adult life for adolescents with severe and multiple disabilities?

What four features characterize successful inclusive education for students with severe and multiple disabilities?

What are four bioethical dilemmas that may have an impact on people with severe and multiple disabilities and their families?

Read

Match these important terms from Chapter Eleven with the correct information.

a. respite care
b. dual diagnosis
c. multiple disabilities
d. holistic approach
e. norm-referenced assessment
f. criterion-referenced assessment
g. academic achievement
h. cognitive functioning
i. Authentic assessment
j. functional assessment
k. ecological assessment
l. multidisciplinary team
m. adaptive fit

11.1 __________ Concomitant impairments such the student can not be accommodated in special education programs solely for one of the impairments.
11.2 __________ Description of persons who have serious emotional problems in conjunction with mental retardation.
11.3 __________ An approach that takes the child into account as a member of the family unit
11.4 __________ Services provided to families of people with severe and multiple disabilities where a trained care-giver periodically assumes responsibility for the individual with severe and multiple disabilities.
11.5 __________ A variety of performance-bases assessments requiring students to demonstrate a response in a real-life conflict
11.6 __________ Assessment with an ecological emphasis that examines the process of learning while focusing on independent living skills.
11.7 __________ Another name for functional assessment..
11.8 __________ Compatibility between demands of a task and needs and abilities of the individual.
11.9 __________ A group comprised of professionals from different fields.
11.10 __________ Level of proficiency in thinking.

11.11 __________ Proficiency in academic areas.

11.12 __________ Assessment by which performance is compared with the average of a group.

11.13 __________ Assessment by which performance is compared to a specific level.

Reflect

Here's another opportunity to test yourself. Can you match these items quickly and correctly?

a. .0002 percent
b. 107,763
c. dual sensory impairment
d. ranges from .1% to 1%
e. multidisciplinary team
f. 1,604
g. 14,000
h. testing

11.14 __________ Approximate number of individuals in U.S. identified as deaf-blind.

11.15 __________ System by which administration and scoring have been refined into a specified, prescribed routine to assure that the process is constant.

11.16 __________ Group responsible for determining the most appropriate educational program and environment for the student.

11.17 __________ Number of students ages 6-21 labeled as *deaf-blind.*

11.18 __________ Estimated number of students served under the label *multiple disabilities.*

11.19 __________ Estimated proportion of students with severe and multiple disabilities served under IDEA.

11.20 __________ People who are deaf-blind.

11.21 __________ Estimated prevalence of severe and multiple disabilities.

Recite

Complete the sentences with words from Chapter Eleven that best fit the blanks. Try to do all eight correctly without reviewing the chapter.

11.22 Historically, terminology associated with severe disabilities communicated a sense of despair and ____________.

11.23 The TASH definition of severe disabilities emphasizes the need for "extensive ongoing __________" in life activities.

11.24 Individuals with severe disabilities may be ___________ under any one of IDEA's categories.

11.25 Most identifiable causes of severe and mental retardation are __________ in origin.

11.26 Intellectual functioning for persons who are deaf-blind may range from normal or ___________ to severe mental retardation.

11.27 Self-determination presumes that student ____________ and needs are taken into account in developing educational objectives.

11.28 For students with severe and multiple disabilities, problems are generally evident at _________.

11.29 Students with severe and multiple disabilities may have severe language and problems.

Review

Choose the best of four possible answers. These questions are a helpful review and a good indication of your grasp of the content.

11.30 Which of the following is not a disability category under IDEA?
- a. Multiple disabilities
- b. Deafness-blindness
- c. Severe disabilities
- d. Autism

11.31 Dual diagnosis involves persons who
- a. have mental retardation and emotional disturbance
- b. vision loss and learning disabilites
- c. hearing loss and cerebral palsy
- d. autism and other health impairments

11.32 Dual sensory impairments involves people who have:
- a. mental retardation as a primary symptom
- b. mental retardation and serious emotional disturbance
- c. severe communication deficits
- d. cerebral palsy and Deafness

11.33 For students with severe disabilities, educators need to build upon which of the following assumptions?
   a. Learning is highly unlikely and the focus should be care and management
   b. There are few similarities between these students and their typical peers
   c. Life functioning seldom improves
   d. Nonc of the above

11.34 Effective programs for infants and toddlers with severe and multiple disabilities are
   a always facility-bases.
   b. characterized by removing the child from the family
   c. child and family-centered
   d. child centered with limited family involvement

11.35 Developmentally appropriate practice (DAP) emphasizes
   a. age-appropriate child exploration and play
   b. academic curricula
   c. instruction consistent with the mental age of the child
   d none of the above.

11.36 Quality programs for elementary-age students with severe disabilities are characterized by
   a. taking into account student preferences and needs
   b. limited parent involvement
   c. isolated skill development
   d. all of the above

11.37 Which is used to analyze a student's individual strengths and weaknesses in different areas, and to indicate the difference between performance areas?
   a. Interindividual assessment
   b. Intraindividual assessment
   c. Norm-referenced assessment
   d. Standardized assessment

11.38 Which of the following is an example of assistive technology?
   a. Wheelchair
   b. Assistance in choosing and using a wheelchair
   c. Computers
   d. All of the above

11.39 Genetic engineering may be seen as a means to
   a. perfect human beings
   b. conquer disease
   c. reducing human suffering
   d. all of the above

11.40 The role of genetic counselor is to
   a. be a moral advisor
   b. remain neutral and give information
   c. communicate personal beliefs
   d. all of the above

11.41 The definition of severe disabilities proposed by The Association for Persons with Severe Handicaps (TASH) focuses on
   a. adaptive fit
   b. children between the ages of birth and 21 years of age
   c. the need for intermittent supports
   d. all of the above

11.42 Professionals have perceived that concomitant visual and hearing loss may result in
   a. functional retardation
   b. average intelligence with severe communication deficits
   c. the lack of ability to initiate or respond to appropriate interactions with others
   d. all of the above

11.43 By definition individuals with serious emotional disturbance are
   a. also severely mentally retarded
   b. not retarded
   c. both retarded and learning disabled
   d. retarded with concomitant physical disabilities

11.44 Most severe and multiple disabilities are evident
   a. in utero
   b. at birth
   c. within the first five years of life
   d. upon entering grade school

11.45 Successful efforts to include students with severe and multiple disabilities utilize
   a. highly trained teachers
   b. systematic organization of opportunities for interaction
   c. specific instruction to increase the competence of students with severe disabilities
   d. all of the above

11.46 The purpose of the Human Genome Project was to
   a. determine the sequence of the 3 billion chemical base pairs in DNA
   b. provide information so that parents would know when selective abortion was appropriate
   c. enable genetic counseling to be completely objective
   d. facilitate the development of genetic engineering to perfect human life

ANSWER KEY FOR CHAPTER ELEVEN

READ

11.1 c
11.2 b
11.3 d
11.4 a
11.5 i
11.6 j
11.7 k
11.8 m
11.9 l
11.10 h
11.11 g
11.12 e
11.13 f

REFLECT

11.14 g
11.15 h
11.16 e
11.17 f
11.18 b
11.19 a
11.20 c
11.21 d

RECITE

11.22 hopelessness
11.23 support
11.24 subsumed
11.25 genetic
11.26 gifted
11.27 preferences
11.28 birth
11.29 perceptual

REVIEW

11.30 a
11.31 c
11.32 d
11.33 c
11.34 a
11.35 a
11.36 b
11.37 d
11.38 d
11.39 b
11.40 a
11.41 d
11.42 b
11.43 b
11.44 d
11.45 a

Chapter Twelve

People with Autism

Preview

Autism was first recognized as a disability in 1990 by IDEA (Individuals with Disabilities Education Act). Autism is considered one of the most challenging disabilities because it affects normal development in so many areas of function. While there are two different estimated ranges of prevalence for autism, it is agreed that substantially more males than females are affected.

Five characteristics associated with the condition of autism are described: impaired or delayed language, self-stimulation, resistance to changes in routine, intelligence, and learning characteristics.

Historically, the causes of autism have been explored under two broad theoretical perspectives, biological and psychodynamic. Researchers have not identified any single specific causal factor, but research has established genetic causation in autism. Currently, it is accepted is that autism is a behavioral syndrome with multiple biological causes.

The major approaches to treatment include educational intervention, psychological and medical intervention, and behavior management. No one approach has been found universally effective.

A child with autism typically has a significant impact on the family. Families may need assistance and support from many sources in meeting the challenges caused by their child's disability.

Question

Be prepared to answer the following questions.

What four areas of functional challenge are often found in children with autism?

What is the general range of prevalence estimated for autism?

What are six characteristics of children with autism?

What are the two broad theoretical views regarding the causes of autism?

What are the four major treatment approaches for people with autism?

Read

Following are some important terms from the chapter. Pair the correct definition with the appropriate term before you read.

a. echolalia
b. splinter skills
c. self-stimulation
d. perseveration
e. psychodynamic theory

12.1 __________ Continual repetition of a behavior beyond the point at which it is meaningful.

12.2 __________ Direct but meaningless repetition of what another person has said.

12.3 __________ Specific areas of ability that are unexpectedly high compared to other levels of function.

12.4 __________ A view indicating that autism is the result of dysfunctional family interactions.

12.5 __________ An activity/behavior that is self-gratifying.

Reflect

Matching the following terms with the correct definitions is a good way to check your understanding of the material in Chapter Eleven.

a. fragile-X syndrome
b. vermis
c. facilitated communication
d. respite

12.6 __________ A part of the cerebellum that may be related to cognitive malfunctions found in autism.

12.7 __________ Child care provided for the temporary relief of the family of a child with a disability.

12.8 __________ A genetic condition involving damage to chromosomal structure.

12.9 __________ A treatment in which the patient types with the therapist providing physical support through touch.

Recite

Fill in each blank with an appropriate word(s).

12.10 Children with autism are frequently described in terms of their difficulty understanding or expressing _____________.

12.11 The legal definition of autism characterizes it as a "__________ disability significantly affecting verbal and nonverbal communication and social interaction."

12.12 Because not all people with autism are alike, it is more accurate to speak of __________ than it is to characterize the condition.

12.13 The American Psychiatric Association estimates the prevalence of autism at about ____ cases per 10,000.

12.14 Estimates of the gender differences in prevalence of autism suggest that males outnumber females anywhere from 2.1 to 1 to _____.

12.15 Often children with autism who develop language have a limited speaking repertoire, and they fail to use _______ in speech directed at another person.

12.16 Approximately ____ to ____ percent of those with autism exhibit what are known as splinter skills.

12.17 Children/youth with autism often experience difficulty interacting with teachers and other students because of their inability to understand _____.

12.18 From a _____________ perspective, family interactions have been implicated as causal factors in autism.

12.19 Thus far researchers have not identified any ________ specific factor that causes autism.

Review

Select the most correct of the four answers listed for each item. Completing this exercise without referring to the text will be a good check of your comprehension.

12.20 The APA estimates the prevalence of autism as about _____ cases per 10,000.
- a. 11 to 15
- b. 5
- c. 10 to 14
- d. 2 to 4

12.21 Many children with autism exhibit low intellectual function, with about percent of them having measured IQs below 70.
a. 90
b. 75
c. 60
d. 50

12.22 One quality that students with autism often possess that may be used to advantage by teachers and therapists is
a. their ability to perseverate
b. their splinter skills
c. their echolalia
d. their enjoyment of routine

12.23 One suspected cause of autism is fragile-X syndrome, which is a condition involving
a. central nervous system damage or impairment
b. damage to the chromosome structure
c. stereotyped self-stimulation
d. restricted behavioral repertoires

12.24 According to the text, it is vital that an IEP for a student with autism have a central component of
a. communication and social skills
b. mobility and orientation training
c. long term memory and neurological development
d. verbal and reasoning skills

12.25 Many high-functioning students with autism who have some language interpret speech literally; therefore, it is important for teachers to avoid
a. telling or reading fairy tales
b. expressing strong feelings
c. slang, idioms, and sarcasm
d. ethnic jokes

12.26 Facilitated communication, a controversial treatment for people with autism, has emphasized
a. the involvement of parents
b. self-directed behavior management
c. improving survival skills
d. the therapist providing physical support

12.27 The label *autism* was taken from the Greek *autos*, to reflect these individuals'
a. robot-like mannerisms
b. quick and rigid patterns of movement
c. extreme self-absorptions, detachment from the world around them
d. intense fear of automobiles

12.28 The Individuals with Disabilities Education Act of 1990 includes in the characteristics of autism
a. engagement in repetitive activities
b. serious emotional disturbance
c. desire for change in daily routines
d. co-dependency

12.29 Children and youths with autism are frequently described as
a. being a nuisance around strangers
b. forming attachments to people
c. being extremely sensitive to others
d. avoiding direct eye contact

12.30 The description *resistant to change* refers to an individual who
a. does not like the furniture to be arranged in the same manner for extended time periods
b. pays attention to the exact route taken when driving to school
c. likes to try different clothing ensembles
d. hates to carry change and prefers dollar bills

12.31 The school performance of students with autism may be described as
a. uneven within and between skill areas
b. consistent
c. focused on general concepts
d. static

12.32 Under the I.D.E.A., students with autism are entitled to a free and appropriate education in a
a. special school
b. regular education classroom
c. separate classroom
d. least restrictive environment

12.33 Behavioral treatment has been used effectively for
a. curing behavior problems
b. curing autism
c. teaching language development and social skills
d. teaching social studies and composition

12.34 Which of the following characteristics may suggest to parents that their infant has autism?
  a. intense need for physical contact
  b. extreme staring at others
  c. rigid when held
  d. excessive random crying

12.35 Echolalia refers to speech patterns in which the youngster
  a. repeats back only what has been said to them
  b. responds to questions which have been repeated several times
  c. responds to individuals who they see repeatedly
  d. emotionally echoes words in a high-pitched voice

12.36 Sometimes, people with autism who develop language
  a. are reflective in their responses
  b. use rapid and emotional speech patterns
  c. have a diverse speaking repertoire
  d. appear to use speech as self stimulation

ANSWER KEY FOR CHAPTER TWELVE

READ	
12.1	d
12.2	a
12.3	b
12.4	e
12.5	c

REFLECT	
12.6	b
12.7	d
12.8	a
12.9	c

RECITE	
12.10	emotion
12.11	developmental
12.12	characteristics
12.13	five
12.14	4 to 1
12.15	pronouns
12.16	10 to 15
12.17	social cues
12.18	psychodynamic
12.19	single

REVIEW	
12.20	b
12.21	b
12.22	d
12.23	b
12.24	a
12.25	c
12.26	d
12.27	c
12.28	a
12.29	d
12.30	b
12.31	a
12.32	d
12.33	c
12.34	c
12.35	a
12.36	d

Chapter Thirteen

People with Traumatic and Acquired Brain Injury

Preview

This chapter begins with medical and educational definitions (IDEA) of traumatic brain injury (TBI) and an explanation of acquired brain injury (ABI). The prevalence of these conditions is then reported.

The most salient characteristics of individuals with TBI are presented. Following is a discussion of the most common causes of TBI.

The various types of educational supports and services for people with traumatic brain injury or acquired brain injury are described. The chapter concludes with an explanation of medical and psychological services available to individuals with TBI.

Read

Following are some of the key terms used in Chapter Thirteen. Match each term with the phrase that most closely describes it. Please complete this exercise before reading the chapter.

a. traumatic brain injury
b. primary damage
c. secondary damage
d. automobile accidents
e. fall from a short distance
f. transition liaison
g. concussion
h. contusion

13.1 __________ Develops over time as the brain responds to the initial trauma.
13.2 __________ The most common closed-head injury.
13.3 __________ A direct outcome of the initial impact to the brain.
13.4 __________ Characterized by extensive damage to the brain, including bleeding, swelling, and bruising.
13.5 __________ Rapid acceleration and deceleration of the brain, including shearing of nerve fibers, . . ., and edema.
13.6 __________ The most common source of brain injury across all ages.
13.7 __________ One who ensures that parents and teachers are adequately prepared to work with the child with TBI.
13.8 __________ The most common cause of brain injury for small children.

Reflect

This exercise allows you to practice recalling important ideas that you have recently read. As above, please match the term with the most appropriate phrase.

a. acquired brain injury
b. 5 million
c. expressive aphasia
d. basilar fracture
e. epidural hematoma
f. subdural hematoma

13.9 __________ Bleeding caused by damage to tiny veins that draw blood from the outer layer of the brain.

13.10 __________ Refers to both traumatic brain injuries and nontraumatic brain injuries.

13.11 __________ A fracture at the base of the skull.

13.12 __________ An inability to express one's own thoughts and desires.

13.13 __________ Bleeding caused by damage to an artery between the brain and the skull.

13.14 __________ Approximate number of people in the United States living with TBI.

Recite

As you recall, here you are to supply a word in order to make sense out of a statement. More than one word may make sense. In comparing your response to the one found in the key, be most concerned with how much sense your answer makes.

13.15 Injuries that do not involve _________ of the skull are referred to as closed-head or generalized head injuries.

13.16 Open-head or _____ injuries involve penetration of the skull.

13.17 There is a dramatic increase in the frequency of acquired brain injuries during the __________ years.

13.18 As a rule, boys are two to ____ times more likely than girls to sustain serious head injuries.

13.19 Neuromotor problems may involve poor_________ coordination.

13.20 The severity and nature of complications and the eventual outcomes of the trauma are directly related to the ________ and degree of injury to the brain.

13.21 It is not uncommon for some students to improve dramatically in the first ______following their injuries.

13.22 Cooperation and __________ are the key factors in achieving success with individual with brain injuries.

Review

This is a great opportunity to review many of the major points found in Chapter Thirteen. By doing well on this exercise you should do well on an exam covering this material.

13.23 Open and closed head injuries may cause impairments in
- a. cognition, language, and memory
- b. attention, reasoning, and abstract thinking
- c. sensory, perceptual, and motor abilities
- d. all of the above

13.24 In order to receive special education services, the child or youth with head trauma must have an injury that
- a. is life-threatening
- b. seriously impairs their ability to relate to others
- c. profoundly impacts their physical functioning
- d. significantly influences their educational performance

13.25 Acquired brain injury (ABI) is a relatively new term. It refers to injuries derived from
- a. strokes and other vascular accidents
- b. infectious diseases
- c. hangings or near drownings
- d. all of the above

13.26 The problems of TBI or ABI are evident primarily in four, overlapping areas
- a. cognitive, speech and language, social and behavioral, and neuromotor and physical functioning
- b. cognitive, speech, behavior, and neuromotor functioning
- c. cognitive, language, social, and physical functioning
- d. cognitive, linguistic, behavioral, and neuromotor functioning

13.27 "High demand" instructional settings or anxiety producing social situations
a. may lessen the presence of expressive aphasia in children and adults
b. may increase the presence of expressive aphasia in children and adults
c. will have no affect on expressive aphasia in children and adults
d. none of the above

13.28 For many individuals, TBI or ABI produce
a. significant changes in their personalities
b. functional changes in their temperaments
c. profound changes in their dispositions for certain activities, and their behaviors
d. all of the above

13.29 For small children, the most common cause of TBI is
a. automobile accidents
b. short falls
c. shaking
d. physical abuse

13.30 Often the first signs of brain injury manifest themselves
a. in a coma
b. in impaired speech
c. in impaired vision
d. in impaired neuromotor fuctioning

13.31 Injuries to the lower back part of the head are
a. easily detected at the injury site
b. partially troublesome as they may set the stage for serious infections
c. easily treated at the injury site
d. none of the above

13.32 The first stage of intervention for traumatic brain injury involves
a. orienting the child, and delivering appropriate psychological interventions
b. treating swelling and bleeding, minimizing complications, and reducing the level of coma
c. checking for age-appropriate skills and behaviors
d. providing appropriate physical therapy

13.33 Many youth and adults return to their homes, schools, or employment settings
a. as vastly different individuals
b. with the same personalities and temperaments
c. with slightly different personalities and temperaments
d. none of the above

13.34 Unfortunately, many children and youth with brain injuries exit hospitals or rehabilitation settings

a. without adequate medical support for their resultant injuries
b. without adequate preparation for their home and school environments
c. without adequate physical therapy services
d. without adequate essential psychological services

13.35 Educational intervention are directed at

a. improving students' general problem solving and planning behaviors
b. developing social behaviors and improving initiative taking
c. restoring or learning expressive and receptive language skills
d. all of the above

13.36 Behavioral effects of TBI include

a. decreased irritability and emotionality insensitivity to others
b. slightly elevated motivation and judgment
c. an inability to restrict socially inappropriate behaviors
d. appropriate thresholds for frustration and inconveniences

ANSWER KEY FOR CHAPTER THIRTEEN

READ

13.1 c
13.2 g
13.3 b
13.4 h
13.5 a
13.6 d
13.7 f
13.8 e

REFLECT

13.9 f
13.10 a
13.11 d
13.12 c
13.13 e
13.14 b

RECITE

13.15 penetration
13.16 focal
13.17 adolescent
13.18 three
13.19 eye-hand
13.20 location
13.21 year
13.22 collaboration

REVIEW

13.23 d
13.24 d
13.25 d
13.26 a
13.27 b
13.28 d
13.29 b
13.30 a
13.31 b
13.32 b
13.33 a
13.34 b
13.35 d
13.36 c

Chapter Fourteen

People with Hearing Loss

Preview

This chapter covers characteristics, causes, assessment and intervention strategies for individuals with hearing loss. The authors supply definitions and classifications of hearing loss, along with statistics associated with the prevalence of hearing impairments. The hearing process is described, including details of the outer, middle, and inner ear.

The authors explain general characteristics of people with hearing loss: intelligence, speech and language skills, educational achievement, and social development. Because they experience difficulty in learning speech and language, people with severe hearing loss must overcome many barriers in order to communicate with the hearing world. Adjustment to the hearing world, and the deaf culture, are also discussed.

The causes of hearing loss are examined and explained under two general classification approaches: (1) congenital or acquired and (2) central or peripheral. Peripheral hearing loss, the most common, is further classified into conductive, sensorineural, or mixed hearing loss.

The four common approaches to teaching communication skills are explained. Rationale for each approach is presented. The chapter also describes the professionals involved in assessment and intervention, and it explains the services of the medical, social, and educational fields. Perspectives on deafness are changing in a radical way.

Question

As you read the chapter, look for the answers to the following questions:

How is sound transmitted through the ear?

What is the distinction between the terms *deaf* and *hard-of-hearing*?

Why is it important to consider age of onset and anatomical site when defining a hearing loss?

What are the causes and estimated prevalence of hearing loss?

What are the basic intellectual, linguistic, educational, and social characteristics of people who are deaf or hard of hearing?

What are four approaches to teaching communication skills to people with a hearing loss?

How are closed-captioned television and computer-assisted instruction used to help people who have a hearing loss?

Why is early detection of a hearing loss so important?

What is the distinction between an otologist and audiologist?

What factors may impede the social integration of people who are deaf into the hearing world?

Read

These are important terms you should know from Chapter Fourteen. Match them with their meanings.

a. audition
b. eustachian tube
c. ossicular chain
d. cochlea
e. Corti's organ
f. vestibular mechanism
g. hertz
h. deaf
i. hard-of-hearing
j. prelingual losss
k. postlingual loss
l. conductive loss
m. sensorineural loss
n. mixed loss

14.1 ________ Three small bones.
14.2 ________ Cycles per second.
14.3 ________ Functional use of residual hearing.
14.4 ________ Area containing semicircular canals that control balance.
14.5 ________ Organ that lies in front of the vestibule.
14.6 ________ The act or sense of hearing.
14.7 ________ Condition in which hearing cannot be used for acquiring new information.
14.8 ________ Organ that equalizes air pressure on the ear drum with outside air pressure.
14.9 ________ Organ that translates vibration into nerve impulses.
14.10 ________ Loss of volume.
14.11 ________ Loss from conductive and sensorineural losses.
14.12 ________ Loss prior to the age of two.

14.13 ________ Loss that occurs after speech development.
14.14 ________ Loss from an abnormal sense organ and a damaged auditory nerve.

Doing well? Here are more to help you learn the material.

o. audiologist
p. otologist
q. audiometer
r. sign language
s. finger-spelling
t. otosclerosis
u. tinnitus
v. atresia
w. fenestration
x. stapedectomy
y. myringoplasty
z. cued speech
aa. closed-caption television
bb. C-print
cc. telecommunication devices for the deaf (TDD)
dd. teletypewriter and printer

14.15 ________ Condition in which the stapes is unable to function properly.
14.16 ________ Reconstruction of the ear drum.
14.17 ________ Replacement of a fixed stapes with a prosthetic device.
14.18 ________ Impairment suffered by victims of otosclerosis.
14.19 ________ Major cause of congenital conductive disorders.
14.20 ________ Process that creates a new opening in the ear.
14.21 ________ Communication system combining hand signals and speech reading.
14.22 ________ Technology that converts typed letters into an electric signal through a modem.
14.23 ________ Device used to detect a person's response to sound stimuli.
14.24 ________ Technology that uses line-21 system.
14.25 ________ Computer system providing real-time translations of the spoken word.
14.26 ________ Physician concerned with the hearing organ and its diseases.
14.27 ________ A language consisting of hand movements that communicate whole words.
14.28 ________ Specialist concerned with the sociological and educational impact of a hearing loss.
14.29 ________ Technology that sends, receives, and prints messages.
14.30 ________ Manual communication in which each letter of a word is formed.

Reflect

Here's another review opportunity.

a. violin string
b. external ear
c. middle ear
d. inner ear
e. ASL
f. bicultural-bilingual approach
g. conductive loss
h. cerebral cortex dysfunction
i. auditory approach
j. oral approach
k. manual approach

14.31 ________ System that involves amplified sound and residual hearing.
14.32 ________ System that uses signs.
14.33 ________ Sign language that is not a form of English.
14.34 ________ Central auditory problem.
14.35 ________ Source of sound waves.
14.36 ________ Cochlea, Corti's organ, vestibular mechanism.
14.37 ________ Belief that ASL is the primary language.
14.38 ________ Peripheral auditory problem.
14.39 ________ System that involves amplified sound, residual hearing, speech reading, writing, and motokinesthetic speech training.
14.40 ________ Auricle, pinna, and meatus.
14.41 ________ Hammer, anvil, and stirrup.

Recite

Check what you have learned. Try to fill in the blanks without referring to the book.

14.42 Although air is the most common carrier, _____ can also be carried by metal, water or other substances.

14.43 The _____ collects sound waves and funnels them into the ear canal.

14.44 Age of onset is critical in determining the type and extent of _____ necessary to minimize the effects of a hearing loss.

14.45 The majority of people with a hearing loss are able to use ____________as the primary mode for language acquisition.

14.46 An ______________ evaluation is intended to measure the degree of hearing loss in an individual.

14.47 The causes of ______ percent of all hearing losses are unknown.

14.48 A prenatal disease known as ______ causes destruction of the capsular bone in the middle ear.

14.49 Prevention of hearing disorders is a primary concern of a ______ specialist.

Review

See if you can answer these correctly. This exercise will help at test time!

14.50 The meatus is

a. a cartilage structure on the side of the head
b. the eardrum
c. one of three ligaments
d. the external ear canal

14.51 The structure that extends between the throat and the middle ear cavity is the

a. eustachian tube
b. vestibular mechanism
c. Corti's organ
d. cochlea

14.52 The leading cause of acquired sensorineural hearing loss is

a. meningitis
b. allergies
c. occupational noise
d. otitis media

14.53 The vestibular mechanism

a. translates vibration into nerve impulses
b. equalizes air pressure on the eardrum
c. collects sound
d. helps maintain balance

14.54 Which type of hearing loss results from poor conduction of sound along passages to the inner ear?

a. Mixed loss
b. Audioneural loss
c. Sensorineural loss
d. Conductive loss

14.55 Research on the intelligence of people with a hearing disorder suggests that

a. intellectual development is more a function of language development than of cognitive ability
b. intellectual development is significantly delayed
c. patterns of intellectual development are inconsistent with the normal sequence
d. intellectual functioning of this population cannot be measured

14.56 Which academic area is most affected by a hearing loss?

a. Writing
b. Arithmetic
c. Reading
d. Science

14.57 What is the effect of a mild hearing loss on speech and language development?

a. Effects on speech and language are minimal.
b. Language is acquired through lip reading.
c. Sound production is low in intelligibility.
d. Language delays often result.

14.58 How many types of hereditary hearing loss are known?

a. 360
b. more than 200
c. 50
d. less than 100

14.59 Which postnatal infection, affecting the brain and spinal cord, is associated with severe hearing disorders in children?

a. Influenza
b. Bronchitis
c. Meningitis
d. Jaundice

14.60 In order to meet the needs of hearing impaired students, educational programs are becoming more

a. general
b. specialized
c. group oriented
d. individualized

14.61 The total communication approach to teaching employs

a. residual hearing and speech reading only
b. the isolated use of speech reading
c. sign language
d. a combination of communication approaches

14.62 The Individuals with Disabilities Education Act (IDEA) defines deafness as a hearing impairment which is so severe that

a. a child is unable to process linguistic information through hearing
b. a child cannot process information through hearing with or without amplification
c. a child's educational performance is adversely affected
d. all of the above

14.63 The age of onset is critical in determining

a. the type of hearing loss
b. the amount of the individual's residual hearing
c. the cause of a hearing loss
d. the type and extent of intervention necessary to minimize the effect of the hearing loss

14.64 A conductive hearing loss may result in

a. distorted pitches
b. reduction or loss of loudness
c. the inability to hear sounds of certain pitches
d. tinnitus

14.65 Which of the following types of hearing loss poses the greatest challenge for the individual in adequately communicating?

a. Congenital deafness
b. Acquired sensorineural loss
c. Otitis media
d. Acquired conductive loss

14.66 Of the 28 million people in the United States,

a. 45% are under the age of 17.is a powerful motivator
b. 11 million have irreversible hearing loss
c. women are more likely than men to have hearing loss
d. all of the above

14.67 In comparison to hearing peers, students with a hearing loss are in reading achievement

a. below average in both areas
b. about the same in both areas
c. above average in both areas
d. virtually indistinguishable

14.68 In the area of social development, children with a hearing loss

a. appear to be less socially mature
b. are more assertive than individuals with normal hearing
c. exhibit significant behavior problems in the school environment
d. typically have high self-esteem

14.69 The delivery of educational services to students with hearing loss under Public Law 99-457 demonstrates an expanding emphasis on

a. early identification and intervention
b. separate facilities for students who are deaf
c. employment education
d. related medical services

ANSWER KEY FOR CHAPTER FOURTEEN

READ

14.1	c
14.2	g
14.3	i
14.4	f
14.5	d
14.6	a
14.7	h
14.8	b
14.9	e
14.10	l
14.11	n
14.12	j
14.13	k
14.14	m
14.15	t
14.16	y
14.17	x
14.18	u
14.19	v
14.20	w
14.21	z
14.22	dd
14.23	q
14.24	aa
14.25	bb
14.26	p
14.27	r
14.28	o
14.29	cc
14.30	s

REFLECT

14.31	i
14.32	k
14.33	e
14.34	h
14.35	a
14.36	d
14.37	f
14.38	g
14.39	j
14.40	b
14.41	c

RECITE

14.42	vibrations
14.43	auricle
14.44	intervention
14.45	speech
14.46	audiometric
14.47	25
14.48	otosclerosis
14.49	genetics

REVIEW

14.50	d
14.51	a
14.52	c
14.53	d
14.54	d
14.55	a
14.56	c
14.57	c
14.58	b
14.59	c
14.60	d
14.61	d
14.62	d
14.63	d
14.64	b
14.65	a
14.66	b
14.67	a
14.68	a
14.69	a

Chapter Fifteen

People with Vision Loss

Preview

Vision links an individual to the world, helping him or her to gain information beyond the range of other senses and to integrate information acquired through hearing, touch, smell, and taste. The way in which visual stimuli are perceived shapes a person's interaction with and reactions to the environment and provides a foundation for developing a more complex learning structure.

This chapter defines vision loss from different perspectives. The medical and legal professions base their definitions on visual acuity and field of vision. The education profession focuses on a student's ability to use vision as an avenue for learning.

Vision loss is classified in the chapter according to the anatomical site of the problem: impairment of the refractive structures of the eye, muscle anomalies in the visual system, or problems in the receptive structures of the eye.

In explaining the characteristics of people with vision loss, Chapter Fifteen examines six areas: intelligence, speech and language skills, academic achievement, social development, orientation and mobility, and perceptual-motor development. The varied causes of loss of vision are commonly categorized as genetically determined or acquired disorders.

Educators concern themselves with assessment, placement, mobility training, daily living skills, instructional content, and training in alternative communication media. Medical, social, and educational services are all involved in assessment and intervention strategies. The medical profession focuses on prevention and treatment of impairments; social services promote social adjustment and community participation.

Questions

While studying Chapter Fifteen, you should anticipate answers to these questions:

Why is it important to understand the process of vision and know the physical components of the eye?

What is the distinction between an individual who is blind and one who is partially sighted?

What are the distinctions between refractive eye problems, muscle disorders, and receptive eye problems?

What are the estimated causes and prevalence rates for vision loss?

In what ways may a vision loss affect intelligence, speech and language skills, educational achievement, social development, orientation and mobility, and perceptual-motor development?

What is a functional approach to assessment for students with vision loss?

What two essential content areas should be included in an educational program for students with vision loss?

In what ways may communication media facilitate learning for people with vision loss?

What is the range of educational services available to students with vision loss?

What steps can be taken to prevent and medically treat vision loss?

Why is the availability of appropriate mental health services important for people with vision loss?

Read

Here's the first group of terms from Chapter Fifteen for you to match with their meanings. If you do well with both sections, you show that you know the material.

a. optic nerve
b. cornea
c. pupil
d. iris
e. retina
f. blind
g. partially sighted
h. visual acuity
i. field of vision
j. educational blindness
k. sight conservation
l. verbalisms
m. braille
n. perceptual-motor

15.1 _____ Muscle that adjusts the size of the pupil.
15.2 _____ Component that consists of light-sensitive cells.
15.3 _____ Term for which the definition varies according to a medical-legal or educational orientation.
15.4 _____ Term that describes students who are able to use vision as a primary source of

learning.

15.5 _____ Component which expands or contracts to control the amount of light entering the eye.

15.6 _____ External covering of the eye.

15.7 _____ Nerve that connects the eye to the visual center of the brain.

15.8 _____ The sharpness or clarity of vision.

15.9 _____ Degree of angle which a person can see without turning the head or moving the eyes.

15.10 _____ Excessive use of speech in which a person uses words that have little personal meaning.

15.11 ____ Position which advocates restricting use of a damaged eye.

15.12 ____ Term that can be defined as whether a student must use braille when reading.

15.13 ____ A language consisting of combinations of six raised dots punched into paper that can be read with the fingertips.

15.14 ____ Term pertaining to a person's ability to interpret stimuli and then respond appropriately.

Here's the second group of terms for you to match with their meanings.

o. refractive problems
p. lens
q. hyperopia
r. myopia
s. astigmatism
t. cataracts
u. muscle disorders of the visual system
v. nystagmus
w. strabismus
x. amblyopia
y. receptive eye problems
z. optic atrophy
aa. retinitis pigmentosa
bb. retinal detachment
cc. retinopathy of prematurity (ROP)
dd. glaucoma

15.15 ____ Component which focuses light rays on the retina.

15.16 ____ Farsightedness.

15.17 ____ Nearsightedness.

15.18 ____ Most common type of visual disorder occurring when light cannot be focused properly on the retina.

15.19 ____ Blurred vision.

15.20 ____ Condition in which the lens becomes opaque.

15.21 ____ Crossed eyes.

15.22 ____ Loss of vision due to muscle imbalance.

15.23 ____ Uncontrolled rapid eye movement.

15.24 ____ Condition which causes inability to maintain focus on an object for even short periods.

15.25 ____ Disorder recognized by high pressure in the eyeball.

15.26 ____ Disorder which can occur when premature infants are administered too much oxygen.

15.27 ____ Condition in which the retina is separated from the choroid and sclera.

15.28 ____ A hereditary condition resulting from a break in the choroid.

15.29 ____ Deterioration of nerve fibers between the retina and the brain.

15.30 ____ Disorder which occurs when there is degeneration of or damage to the retina and the optic nerve.

Reflect

These terms relate to information concerning the causes of visual disorders. If you get all nine, you're doing well.

a. choroid-retinal deterioration
b. retinoblastoma
c. pseudoglioma
d. microphthalmus
e. anophthalmos
f. buphthalmos
g. hydrocephalus
h. genetically determined disorders
i. acquired disorders

15.31 ______________ Disorders that occur prior to, during, or immediately after birth.

15.32 ______________ Disorders that may be caused by hereditary factors.

15.33 ______________ Excess cerebrospinal fluid in the brain.

15.34 ______________ Abnormal distention and enlargement of the eyeball.

15.35 ______________ A malignant tumor in the retina.

15.36 ______________ A nonmalignant intraocular disturbance resulting from the detachment of the retina.

15.37 ______________ A deterioration of the choroid and retina.

15.38 ______________ Absence of the eyeball.

15.39 ______________ Abnormally small eyeball.

Recite

These sentences for you to complete are relevant to assessment and intervention strategies for visual disorders. Review the topic before you begin, then try this section without using the book.

15.40 The _________ labels a person's visual acuity by using an index that refers to the distance at which an object can be recognized.

15.41 A handheld ultrasound travel aid that vibrates at different rates to warn of obstacles in front of the individual is called a ________.

15.42 A __________ is a device that converts infrared light into sound as light beams strike objects.

15.43 A device worn on the head that emits ultrasound and is capable of converting reflections from objects into audible noise is the ________.

15.44 A recent innovation for braille readers that may reduce some of the problems associated with the medium is the _______.

15.45 The _______________ is a device that uses pins as tactile reproductions of printed material.

15.46 The _______________ is a device that converts printed matter into synthetic speech.

15.47 A system of writing that involves combinations of six raised dots is ___________.

Review

These questions will help prepare you for an exam on material from Chapter Fifteen.

15.48 The retina consists of light-sensitive cells that transmit an image to the brain by means of
- a. the optic nerve
- b. visual cells
- c. the iris
- d. the cornea

15.49 The medical-legal definition of blindness includes references to
- a. visual acuity and reading ability
- b. light and motion detection
- c. visual acuity and field of vision
- d. light detection and field of vision

15.50 Educational definitions of blindness focus primarily on the student's ability to use vision as

a. a means of controlling mobility
b. an avenue for increasing intelligence
c. the primary sense
d. an avenue for learning

15.51 What two components are essential to the success of an educational program for a student with a visual impairment?

a. Speech and language training
b. Mobility and orientation training
c. Reading and listening comprehension services
d. Oral expression and handwriting

15.52 People with a vision loss

a. live a deprived socioecomonic and cultural existence
b. are incapable of learning many basic skills
c. can achieve independence and lead satisfying, productive lives
d. believe they are being punished for their sins

15.53 Disorders associated with the receptive structures of the eye occur when there is a degeneration of or damage to the retina and the

a. cornea
b. iris
c. visual center
d. optic nerve

15.54 The only fair way to compare the intellectual capabilities of sighted and blind children is on tasks on which the visual disorder does not interfere with

a. performance
b. mobility
c. reading
d. comprehension

15.55 Children who suffer a high degree of vision loss are at a distinct disadvantage in developing speech and language skills because they are unable to visually associate

a. a word and the sentence containing it
b. a word with the object it represents
c. letters that form words
d. words and their meanings

15.56 A person is considered legally blind if the widest angle of his/her visual field is limited to or less than

a. 10 degrees
b. 20 degrees
c. 30 degrees
d. 40 degrees

15.57 Children who are blind are generally two years older than sighted children in the same grade. Which factor best explains the delayed academic progress of these children?

a. Lower intelligence of blind children.
b. Blind children often enter school at a later age.
c. Lessened mobility of blind children.
d. Heavy reliance on hearing by blind children.

15.58 A vision loss may affect fine motor coordination and interfere with the ability to

a. negotiate a classroom setting
b. develop intelligence
c. manipulate objects
d. read by using braille

15.59 *Sensory compensation*, the notion that blind people have superior senses other than sight, is

a. empirically valid
b. empirically invalid
c. accepted as fact
d. a learned skill

15.60 Eric has 20/30 vision. This means that Eric

a. can see at twenty feet what a normally sighted person can see at thirty feet
b. can see at thirty feet what a normally sighted person can see at twenty feet
c. has a 20 degree field of vision
d. has a 30 degree field of vision

15.61 A person who is partially sighted

a. is unable to benefit from large print books and posters
b. is unable to use vision for learning
c. has visual acuity greater than 20/200, but not greater than 20/70 in the better eye after correction
d. all of the above

15.62 If an individual loses his/her sight after the age of five

a. the social development of the child will be significantly affected
b. a visual frame of reference may be maintained
c. academic achievement will not be affected
d. language development will be negatively affected

15.63 "Verbalisms" refers to
- a. the use of too many verbs in a sentence
- b. the excessive use of speech
- c. the incorrect sequence of words in a sentence
- d. the incorrect choice of verbs for intended meaning

15.64 Jason is having trouble reading instructions that are written on the blackboard. This indicates that his teacher should
- a. move Jason to the front of the room immediately
- b. not require Jason to copy work from the board
- c. schedule Jason for a visual screening test by the school nurse
- d. suggest that Jason eat more carrots

15.65 Historically, most students who were blind received their education in
- a. general education classrooms with supportive services
- b. special education classrooms
- c. residential facilities
- d. their home

15.66 Personal digital assistants (PDAs) are capable of
- a. balancing a checkbook
- b. turning home appliances on and off
- c. maintaining a daily appointment book
- d. all of the above

ANSWER KEY FOR CHAPTER FIFTEEN

READ

15.1	d
15.2	e
15.3	f
15.4	g
15.5	c
15.6	b
15.7	a
15.8	h
15.9	i
15.10	l
15.11	k
15.12	j
15.13	m
15.14	n
15.15	p
15.16	q
15.17	r
15.18	o
15.19	s
15.20	t
15.21	w
15.22	x
15.23	v
15.24	u
15.25	dd
15.26	cc
15.27	bb
15.28	aa
15.29	z
15.30	y

REFLECT

15.31	i
15.32	h
15.33	g
15.34	f
15.35	b
15.36	c
15.37	a
15.38	e
15.39	d

RECITE

15.40	Snellen Test
15.41	Mowat Sensor
15.42	Laser Cane
15.43	Sonicguide
15.44	Mountbat Brailler
15.45	Optacon
15.46	Kurzweil Reading Machine
15.47	braille

REVIEW

15.48	a
15.49	c
15.50	d
15.51	b
15.52	c
15.53	d
15.54	a
15.55	b
15.56	b
15.57	b
15.58	c
15.59	b
15.60	a
15.61	c
15.62	b
15.63	b
15.64	c
15.65	c
15.66	d

Chapter Sixteen

People with Physical and Health Disabilities

Preview

Physical disabilities is a term generally used to refer to impairments that interfere with a person's mobility, coordination, communication, learning, or personal adjustment. This chapter discusses a representative sample of disabling physical conditions, including cerebral palsy, seizure disorders (epilepsy), spina bifida, spinal cord injuries, and muscular dystrophy.

Health disabilities are conditions resulting in "limited strength, vitality or alertness," which are "due to chronic or acute health problems." Such health disabilities significantly alter not only the life of the person who develops one of them, but also the lives of that person's family and friends.

For each major condition the authors furnish details, definitions and concepts. They explain causation, prevalence, and interventions

The chapter also discusses diabetes, cystic fibrosis, sickle cell anemia, human immunodeficiency virus (HIV) and acquired immune deficiency syndrome (AIDS). Other health-relevant conditions, including child abuse, adolescent pregnancy, suicide, and maternal drug and alcohol abuse, are described as well. Current interventions or prevention strategies are explained.

With appropriate and comprehensive treatment, people with physical and/or health disabilities can achieve personal independence and other goals necessary for a full and independent life.

Questions

In reading Chapter Sixteen you will find answers to the following questions:

Why are many individuals with cerebral palsy considered to be multidisabled?

What is spina bifida myelomingocele?

What specific treatments are provided to individuals with spinal-cord injuries?

What are the physical limitations associated with muscular dystrophy?

What steps should be taken to assist infants and children with AIDS?

How should one respond to a person who is experiencing a tonic/clonic seizure?

What three problems may individuals with diabetes eventually experience?

What are present and future interventions used in treating people with cystic fibrosis?

What impact does sickling of cells have on the tissues of the body?

What five factors may contribute to child abuse and neglect?

What factors appear to contribute to the increase in adolescent pregnancy?

What appear to be the major causes of suicide in youth?

What are the potential effects of maternal substance abuse on the developing child?

Read

These terms are important for your understanding of physical and health disabilities. Match them with their correct definition. Some are similar, so read definitions carefully.

a. physical disabilities
b. cerebral palsy
c. contractures
d. spina bifida
e. spina bifida occulta
f. spina bifida cystica
g. spinal cord injuries
h. anemia
i. muscular dystrophy
j. human immunodeficiency virus (HIV)

16.1 ________ A permanent shortening and thickening of muscle fibers.
16.2 ________ A developmental defect of the spinal column.
16.3 ________ A condition in which an oblique slit is present in one or more vertebral structures.
16.4 ________ Bodily impairments that interfere with a person's mobility, coordination, communication, learning, or personal adjustment.
16.5 ________ A group of chronic conditions characterized by motor problems, general physical weakness, lack of coordination, and physical dysfunction.
16.6 ________ A malformation of the spinal column in which a tumor-like sack is produced on the infant's back.
16.7 ________ Injuries in which the spinal cord is traumatized or severed.
16.8 ________ A virus that reduces the immune system functioning--linked to AIDS.
16.9 ________ A group of genetic diseases that are characterized by gradual wasting and weakening of the voluntary skeletal muscle.

16.10 _______ A condition in which there is a deficiency in red blood cells.

Reflect

These terms represent information dealing with cerebral palsy. Match all seven with their correct definitions.

spastic
athetoid
ataxic
500,000
4-5/2000
motor problems, general physical weakness, lack of coordination
premature birth, maternal infection, chronic disease

16.11 _______ Prevalence of CP in the United States.
16.12 _______ Characteristics associated with cerebral palsy.
16.13 _______ May all be sources of CP.
16.14 _______ Children and adults in the U.S. presenting one or more features of CP.
16.15 _______ Characterized by extreme difficulty in controlling both gross and fine motor movements.
16.16 _______ Characterized by involuntary contractions of the muscles which occur when the person attempts to stretch or use various muscle groups.
16.17 _______ Characterized by constant, contorted, twisting motions, particularly in the wrists and fingers.

Recite

Fill the blanks with words relating to physical disabilities. These questions are challenging.

16.18 The paralysis category that involves the legs only is ____________.

16.19 People with physical disabilities are significantly affected by the attitudes and expectations of __________

16.20 Because of its multifaceted nature, ___________________ may require treatment by many different professionals.

16.21 The primary treatment for seizures is ________ drug therapy.

16.22 Physical therapists play an important role in maintaining physical functioning and preventing contractions for people with __________

16.23 After a spinal cord injury once the spine has been stabilized, the __________ process can begin.

16.24 Removing physical barriers such as curbs and steps makes crossing the street and entering buildings much easier for those who travel by ________________.

16.25 Physical therapy includes techniques designed to strengthen muscles, teach muscle relaxation, and optimize __________ function.

Review

Choose the best of the four listed answers. Try to answer all correctly without referring to the text.

16.26 People with cerebral palsy are often considered multihandicapped because
- a. they often score below average on intelligence tests
- b. their Individualized Education Plans (IEPs) are usually complex
- c. they often have a variety of problems varying in degrees of severity
- d. they are usually quadriplegic

16.27 Which type of seizure is characterized by brief periods of inattention, accompanied by rapid eye blinking or head twitching?
- a. Absence seizure
- b. Tonic/clonic seizure
- c. Grand mal seizure
- d. Daydreaming

16.28 What happens to a person's physical condition as muscular dystrophy progresses?
- a. Muscles tighten and become spastic.
- b. Leg muscles are strengthened.
- c. Muscle tissue atrophies and is gradually replaced by fatty tissue.
- d. Bone tissue slowly weakens.

16.29 The socialization and career goals of those with physical disabilities are similar to those of
- a. people with mental retardation
- b. people with learning disabilities
- c. people with multiple disorders
- d. their nondisabled peers

16.30 Most children with spina bifida who have no signs of hydrocephalus have
- a. normal intelligence
- b. abnormal behavior
- c. no paralysis
- d. no apparent disorder

16.31 A paralytic condition involving all four limbs or extremities is classified as
a. paraplegia
b. monoplegia
c. triplegia
d. quadriplegia

16.32 What is the first phase of treatment provided to a person who has suffered a spinal cord injury?
a. Management of shock
b. Instruction in using residual muscle strength
c. Psychiatric treatment
d. Immobilization of the person

16.33 Which is responsible for half of all spinal cord injuries?
a. Motor vehicle accidents
b. Falls
c. Sports-related injuries
d. Injuries at birth

16.34 The IDEA uses the term to describe children with physical disabilities
a. physically impaired
b. orthopedically impaired
c. crippled
d. physically disabled

16.35 One of the major problems experienced by people with muscular dystrophy, which seriously interferes with the person's ability to walk or move, is the development of
a. contractures
b. muscle spasms
c. seizures
d. arthritis

16.36 A mild condition in which a very small slit is present in one or several of the vertebral structures is
a. spina bifida meningocele
b. spina bifida myelomeningocela
c. spina bifida occulta
d. spina bifida cystica

16.37 If a spinal cord injury occurs in the lower back, paralysis will usually be confined to the lower extremities. If the injury occurs in the neck or upper back, the resultant paralysis and effects will usually be
a. in the upper portion of the body
b. less extensive
c. much more extensive
d. negligible

16.38 Which professional is responsible for developing a student's physical skills?
a. A physical therapist
b. A massage therapist
c. A special education teacher
d. An orthopedist

16.39 Disordered metabolism, blindness, cardiovascular disease, and kidney disease are all possible symptoms of
a. asthma
b. diabetes
c. cystic fibrosis
d. AIDS

16.40 Which of the following statements is true about cystic fibrosis?
a. It occurs as the result of an infection
b. It is a disorder of the secretion glands
c. It affects the kidneys, lungs and heart
d. It does not affect the digestive tract

16.41 Which condition causes blockage in microvascular channels that reduces or terminates circulation, and kills tissues by depriving them of blood nutrients and oxygen?
a. AIDS
b. Asthma
c. Sickle cell anemia
d. Diabetes

16.42 Child abuse can be regarded
a. as a means of maladaptive coping by parents
b. as a primary function of poverty
c. as a primary outcome of substance abuse
d. as a primary function of serious psychiatric problems

16.43 Children with AIDS should attend school unless they
a. are subaverage in intellectual functioning
b. exhibit behaviors that are dangerous to others
c. cause fear and mistrust among students and teachers
d. choose not to attend

16.44 Which is advisable when speaking to a friend who is contemplating suicide?
- a. End the conversation abruptly to show it's not an acceptable topic.
- b. Talk freely but not about suicide.
- c. Talk freely about suicide but don't use the word.
- d. Talk freely about suicide and use the word.

16.45 Emily was involved in a skiing accident which resulted in paralysis on the right side of her body. This condition is called
- a. monoplegia
- b. paraplegia
- c. hemiplegia
- d. quadriplegia

16.46 Cystic fibrosis is an inherited, systemic, generalized disease that begins at
- a. birth
- b. childhood
- c. adolescence
- d. conception

16.47 Education for children with cystic fibrosis should occur, in most instances, in a
- a. special school
- b. regular school setting
- c. special education classroom
- d. resource room

16.48 How can teachers and others help abused children make the adjustments necessary for leading happy lives?
- a. Provide highly structured educational and environmental settings.
- b. Establish and maintain strict rules for the child.
- c. Refer abused children to a school counselor.
- d. Provide a stable, positive environment.

16.49 Suicide is generally a culmination of serious and numerous problems. Why do these problems lead to suicide for some adolescents?
- a. They perceive the events as being serious; this is compounded by repeated failure to resolve problems.
- b. Primarily hereditary factors triggered by certain events.
- c. They experience sudden depression disorder.
- d. They react impulsively to typical adolescent problems.

16.50 Recently the communication abilities of children with cerebral palsy have been enhanced through the use of
a. a communication board
b. the teletypewriter
c. the speech synthesizer
d. sign language

16.51 Alice was born with spina bifida. Her legs are paralyzed, and she has difficulty with bowel and bladder control. It is likely that Alice has
a. Spina bifida occulta
b. Spina bifida meningocele
c. Spina bifida mylomeningocele
d. Spina bifida cystica

16.52 The presence of the human immunodeficiency virus (HIV) and/or the presence of antibodies to HIV in a child's blood, along with recurrent bacterial infections, is the definition for
a. leukemia
b. acquired immune deficiency syndrome (AIDS)
c. hemophilia
d. diabetes

16.53 Clusters of behavior that occur in response to abnormal neurochemical activity in the brain are called
a. blackouts
b. seizures
c. delusions
d. hallucinations

16.54 Absence seizures are characterized by
a. verbal outbursts
b. brief periods of inattention
c. irregular breathing
d. increased physical activity

16.55 Diabetes is a condition in which there is
a. an inadequate secretion of insulin
b. an excess of insulin
c. an abnormal decrease of glucose in the blood
d. an excess of glucose in liver and muscles

16.56 A chronic disorder which is a function of abnormal hemoglobin molecules in the red blood cells is
   a. sickle cell anemia
   b. leukemia
   c. juvenile diabetes
   d. cystic fibrosis

16.57 What is the major purpose of hospitalization in cases of child abuse?
   a. To provide a short-term safe environment for the child.
   b. To give the parents respect.
   c. To deal with immediate physical injuries to the child.
   d. To provide a placement for children who have been permanently removed from their parents.

16.58 Children born to mothers aged fifteen or younger may experience
   a. higher rates of birth defects
   b. higher rates of mental retardation
   c. higher rates of central nervous system dysfunctions
   d. all of the above

16.59 Preliminary treatment for preschoolers affected by cocaine centers on
   a. designing highly structured learning environments
   b. participating in therapeutic play groups
   c. creating highly stimulating learning environments
   d. none of the above

ANSWER KEY FOR CHAPTER SIXTEEN

READ

16.1 c
16.2 d
16.3 e
16.4 a
16.5 b
16.6 f
16.7 g
16.8 j
16.9 i
16.10 h

RECITE

16.18	paraplegia
16.19	others
16.20	cerebral palsy
16.21	anticonvulsant
16.22	muscular dystrophy
16.23	rehabilitation
16.24	wheelchair
16.25	physical

REFLECT

16.11 e
16.12 f
16.13 g
16.14 d
16.15 c
16.16 a
16.17 b

REVIEW

16.26 c
16.27 a
16.28 c
16.29 d
16.30 a
16.31 d
16.32 a
16.33 a
16.34 b
16.35 a
16.36 a
16.37 c
16.38 a
16.39 b
16.40 b
16.41 c
16.42 a
16.43 b
16.44 d
16.45 c
16.46 d
16.47 b
16.48 d
16.49 a
16.50 c
16.51 c
16.52 b
16.53 b
16.54 b
16.55 a
16.56 a
16.57 c
16.58 d
16.59 a

Chapter Seventeen

People Who are Gifted, Creative, and Talented

Preview

Gifted, creative and *talented* are terms associated with a group of people who have extraordinary abilities in one or more areas of performance. This chapter begins with a historical look at the study of giftedness and examines research efforts to explore intelligence.

Definitions of giftedness are important since the concept of giftedness that is being used has a profound impact on the kind of education provided to students with exceptional ability. For example, definitions influence the number of students selected for gifted programs, the types of instruments and selection procedures used, the scores one must obtain to qualify for specialized instruction, the types of different education provided, the amount of funding allotted for services, and the types of training required of those who teach gifted and talented programs. Definitions of giftedness are a function of our educational, societal, and political priorities at a given time.

Chapter Seventeen covers the prevalence, characteristics, and origins of giftedness. Gifted people vary significantly in characteristics; they are not a homogeneous group. Techniques of assessment that are explored include teacher nomination, intelligence and achievement tests, and creativity tests.

Intervention strategies focus on helping gifted/talented children and youth to develop their abilities during early childhood, childhood, and adolescence. A number of service delivery systems, such as acceleration, enrichment, special programs and schools, career education, and mentoring, are used to provide differentiated education to gifted and talented students. Parents play a major role in advancing their children's development by providing varied opportunities suited to the child's strengths and interests.

The chapter concludes with a discussion of historically neglected groups, stressing the unique problems that they face.

Questions

Find answers to these questions as you read.

What historical developments are directly related to the measurement of various types of giftedness?

What are six major components of definitions that have been developed to describe giftedness?

What four problems are inherent in accurately describing the characteristics of gifted people?

What are three factors that appear to contribute significantly to the emergence of various forms of giftedness?

What types of assessment are used to identify the various forms of giftedness?

What interventions are used to foster the development of children and adolescents who are gifted?

What are some of the social-emotional needs of students who are gifted?

What are four important aspects of counter conditioning for gifted girls?

What are the eight essential elements of programs for gifted children coming from diverse backgrounds?

Read

These are terms from Chapter Seventeen that you should know. Match them with their correct definitions.

a. gifted, creative, and talented
b. mental age
c. intelligence quotient (IQ)
d. Stanford-Binet Individual Intelligence Scale
e. differentiated education
f. acceleration
g. nature-nurture controversy
h. enrichment
i. mentoring

17.1 ______ Instruction and learning activities that are suited to the capacities and interests of gifted students.
17.2 ______ A process that allows students to achieve at a rate that is consistent with their capacity.
17.3 ______ Educational experiences that enhance gifted students' thinking skills and extend their knowledge in various areas.
17.4 ______ A standardized individual intelligence test.
17.5 ______ A score obtained from an intelligence test that provides a measure of mental ability in relation to age.
17.6 ______ Terms applied to those with extraordinary abilities in one or more areas of performance.

17.7 ______ General mental ability possessed by the average child of a given age.
17.8 ______ An approach that allows gifted students to work directly with professionals.
17.9 ______ The debate regarding respective contributions of heredity and environment to intelligence.

Reflect

Here are more terms and names you need to know. Match them with the correct item.

a. Alfred Binet
b. Binet and Simon
c. Lewis Terman
d. intelligence quotient
e. J. P. Guilford
f. Javits Gifted and Talented Education Act
g. Tannenbaum
h. Sternberg

17.10 ____ Calculated by dividing mental age by chronological age times one hundred.
17.11 ____ Saw intelligence as a diverse range of intellectual and creative abilities.
17.12 ____ Developed the concept and measurement of mental age.
17.13 ____ Published Stanford-Binet Individual Intelligence Scale and developed the term intelligence quotient.
17.14 ____ Constructed the first developmental assessment scale for children.
17.15 ____ Basis for government support of gifted/talented.
17.16 ____ Defined 2 types of gifted individuals: perfomers and producers
17.17 ____ Triarchic theory of human intelligence.

Recite

Complete the sentences with words from Chapter Sixteen.

17.18 Qualified assessment personnel should identify ________ individuals.

17.19 Gifted youngsters may demonstrate their abilities in a variety of ________.

17.20 The theory of multiple intelligences says there are ___________ types of intelligences.

17.21 In order to realize their full intellectual and creative potential, gifted children need special ________ opportunities.

17.22 Gifted individuals vary significantly on a wide range of characteristics. They are not a ________ group.

17.23 Many of the early studies of gifted people gave a __________view of giftedness.

17.24 Genetic endowment certainly contributes to the presence of ________________.

17.25 Gifted women may lack models or mentors with whom they may _____________.

17.26 At the present time few instruments are capable of assessing the abilities of those who are substantially ______ from the core culture.

17.27 All children should have the opportunity to realize their creative and intellectual ___________.

Review

For each item choose the best of the four answers listed. If you get them all right without using your book, you are talented!

17.28 Grade skipping, condensed programs, rapid progress, and early entry to college are examples of which educational approach for gifted students?
- a. Special school
- b. Enrichment
- c. Acceleration
- d. Career exploration

17.29 In order to realize their full intellectual and creative potential, gifted children need
- a. to be separated from normal children
- b. special education opportunities
- c. constant verbal reinforcement
- d. little stimulation

17.30 A conceptualization of giftedness proposed by Gagne centers on
- a. catalysts that have both positive and negative impacts
- b. a pyramid of talent development
- c. two types of gifted individuals, performers, and producers
- d. none of the above

17.31 What contributes to the presence of giftedness?
- a. Heredity
- b. Environmental factors
- c. An interaction of innate ability and appropriate environmental stimulation
- d. Neither heredity nor environmental factors

17.32 In pursuing various careers and professional options, gifted women may lack
a. adequate models or mentors
b. sufficient motivation
c. necessary talents and skills
d. support from peers

17.33 The availability of specialized educational services for those identified as gifted is
a. mandated by federal laws
b. found only in private schools
c. found only in special schools
d. not mandated by federal laws

17.34 Which contributes most to the difficulty of determining the prevalence of giftedness?
a. Variable results from testing
b. Variable definitions of giftedness
c. The eagerness of parents to have their children labeled gifted
d. Withdrawn behavior among gifted children

17.35 Capacities associated with creativity include
a. elaboration, transformation, and visualization
b. enumeration, transformation, and visualization
c. intellectualization, transformation, and visualization
d. all of the above

17.36 The first developmental assessment scale created by Binet in the early 1900's was used to identify
a. students who were gifted
b. students with specific learning needs
c. students who were mentally retarded
d. students with emotional problems

17.37 Given the present multifaceted definitions of giftedness, we must conclude that gifted people are
a. a homogeneous population
b. a heterogeneous population
c. easily identified
d. a large percentage of the population

17.38 The first step in identifying gifted people is generally known as

a. screening
b. selection
c. nomination
d. identification

17.39 Which basic criterion has been used historically to place students in gifted programs?

a. Achievement test scores
b. Mental age level
c. IQ score
d. Teacher nomination

17.40 Which educational approach is used most commonly in serving gifted students?

a. The special school
b. Enrichment
c. Acceleration
d. Career exploration

17.41 Currently, _______ of the school population may be identified as gifted.

a. 3-5
b. 5-10
c. 3-20
d. 2-8

17.42 The identification process for giftedness is ideally directed at

a. creating standardized cut-off scores
b. giving multiple intelligence tests
c. identifying needs and potentials
d. using several creativity measures

17.43 Josh is an extremely bright third grade student who always finishes his work quickly, but accurately. When he has finished, he disturbs his classmates, refuses to stay in his seat, and is quite distracting. Josh's teacher has never considered that he might be a gifted student. This might be true because teachers are more likely to identify students who are _________ as gifted students.

a. bright, but not too disruptive
b. cooperative
c. attractive
d. motivated

17.44 The enrichment method for educating gifted students been criticized by professionals because

a. it is often used in a superficial fashion to placate parents who demand gifted programming
b. enrichment activities are often devoted to educational trivia
c. enrichment programs often do not have well-delineated objectives
d. all of the above

17.45 According to Silverman, the most damaging aspect of the socialization of girls in relation to giftedness is

a. society's expectation that girls marry and raise children
b. society's emphasis on glamour and femininity
c. society's encouragement of dependence in females
d. society's low expectations for females in mathematics and other related areas

17.46 The procedures used to identify disadvantaged children and youth who are gifted includes

a. considering broader ranges of scores for inclusion in gifted programs
b. peer nomination
c. parent nomination
e. all of the above

17.47 Governors school" and specialized residential high schools provide valuable experiences for gifted, talented, and creative individuals because

a. the curriculum is designed to accommodate individual aptitudes and interests
b. although faculty are not specifically trained to educate students who are gifted, they do attempt to motivate and stimulate students
c. it is preferable for high functioning secondary school students to interact only with individuals of the same ability level
d. all of the above

17.48 Females who are gifted experience the following problem(s)

a. fear of appearing unfeminine
b. stress induced by unrealistic work demands
c. self-imposed, excessively open expectations
d. all of the above

17.49 A factor that is essential in identifying giftedness in individuals with disabling conditions is that

a. students must be given the opportunity to perform tasks that are identical to their nondisabled peers
b. tests used to measure mental ability must be specifically designed for use with students with a disability
c. information about the student's performance must be gathered from multiple sources
d. the family of the student with a disability must agree that their child shows signs of giftedness

17.50 Instructional programs for children and adolescents who are disadvantaged and gifted include

a. teachers who are well trained, who understand learning styles
b. teachers who capitalize on students' interests
c. teachers who maximize students' affective and cognitive capacities
d. all of the above

ANSWER KEY FOR CHAPTER SEVENTEEN

READ

17.1 e
17.2 f
17.3 h
17.4 d
17.5 c
17.6 a
17.7 b
17.8 i
17.9 g

REFLECT

17.10 d
17.11 e
17.12 b
17.13 c
17.14 a
17.15 f
17.16 g
17.17 h

RECITE

17.18 gifted
17.19 domains
17.20 seven
17.21 educational
17.22 homogeneous
17.23 stereotypical
17.24 giftedness
17.25 identify
17.26 different
17.27 potential

REVIEW

17.28 c
17.29 b
17.30 a
17.31 c
17.32 a
17.33 d
17.34 b
17.35 a
17.36 c
17.37 b
17.38 a
17.39 c
17.40 b
17.41 c
17.42 c
17.43 b
17.44 d
17.45 c
17.46 d
17.47 a
17.48 a
17.49 c
17.50 d

NOTES

NOTES

NOTES

NOTES

NOTES

NOTES

NOTES

NOTES

NOTES

NOTES

NOTES

NOTES

NOTES

NOTES

NOTES